ACTION AND KNOWLEDGE

Breaking the Monopoly with Participatory Action-Research

ACTION AND KNOWLEDGE

Breaking the Monopoly with Participatory Action-Research

Edited by

**Orlando Fals-Borda and
Muhammad Anisur Rahman**

**The Apex Press
New York**

**Intermediate Technology Publications
London**

Published by The Apex Press, an imprint of the Council on International and Public Affairs, 777 United Nations Plaza, New York, New York 10017 (212/953-6920)

Published in the United Kingdom by Intermediate Technology Publications, 103-105 Southampton Row, London WC1B 4HH

This book is published simultaneously in Spanish by:

CINEP (Centro de Investigación y Educación Popular), Carrera 5, No. 33-A-08, Bogotá, Colombia

and

CEAAL (Consejo de Educación de Adultos de América Latina), Pérez Valenzuela No. 1632, Santiago 22, Chile

Library of Congress Cataloging-in-Publication Data

Action and knowledge : breaking the monopoly with participatory action research / edited by Orlando Fals-Borda and Muhammad Anisur Rahman.
     p.   cm.
    Includes bibliographical references.
    ISBN 0-945257-31-7
    1. Social sciences—Research—Developing countries. 2. Action research—Developing countries. 3. Social participation—Developing countries. 4. Community development—Developing countries. 5. Decision making, Group—Developing countries. I. Fals-Borda, Orlando. II. Rahman, Md. Anisur (Muhammad Anisur)
H62.5D44A28 1991
300'.7201724—dc20
                            90-24300

ISBN 0-945257-31-7 (U.S.)   ISBN 0-945277-57-0 (U.S. Cloth)
ISBN 1-85339-098-4 (U.K.)

Cover design by Janette Aiello
Typeset and printed in the United States of America

CONTENTS

PREFACE

This book is the result of field work and reflection inspired in Participatory Action-Research (PAR) techniques and philosophy during the last twenty years, when this form of study-and-action was first proposed and tried. The book does not attempt the impossible task of covering the entire field. It does try, however, to underline PAR's main features as we have experienced them, illustrating them in Part II through a handful of process studies, or *vivencias*, from different countries.

Such *vivencias* are expected to show why PAR is a viable approach to face some of the very old problems still experienced in many parts of the world where "development" policies have been tried and found wanting. However, although the crisis of "development" and its discourse is every day more widely felt and discussed, because PAR began much before, the alternative rise of PAR should not be interpreted as a response to it. From the beginning, those who adopted PAR have tried to practice with a radical commitment that has gone beyond usual institutional boundaries, reminiscent of the challenging tradition of Chartists, utopians and other social movements of the nineteenth century.

Therefore, while recognizing that ours is an ancient, permanent task, it is our hope to reach social action groups, grassroots animators, intellectuals and government officials with a constructive message adapted to present needs for social and economic change, and conducive to other options for enlightenment and awakening of common peoples—especially those forgotten, despised or left voiceless by the dominant Establishments. We are concerned with such sociopolitical problems as people's power and struggles, and with cognitive issues, such as those implied in the accumulation of different types of knowledge. The pertinent theoretical discussion is found in Parts I and III, written also with a view to undertake a dialogue with academic scholars and in particular those who consider themselves "post-modern."

We want to express our appreciation to the collaborators of this book and to the many groups that participated in the experiences. Thanks are due also to the director of the Institute of Political and International Studies of the National University of Colombia, Bogotá, and to the chief of the Rural Employment Policies Branch of the International Labour Office, Geneva, for their institutional support of the present work.

Bogotá and Geneva   The Editors
December 1990

PART I
INTRODUCTION

Chapter 1

SOME BASIC INGREDIENTS*

Orlando Fals-Borda

In order to refresh the mind on the methodological components of participatory action-research as practiced in many parts of the world,[1] it is useful to recall from the beginning that PAR is not exclusively research oriented, that it is not only adult education or only sociopolitical action. It encompasses all these aspects together as three stages, or emphases, which are not necessarily consecutive. They may be combined into an experiential methodology, that is, a process of personal and collective behavior occurring within a satisfying and productive cycle of life and labor. This experiential methodology implies the acquisition of serious and reliable knowledge upon which to construct power, or countervailing power, for the poor, oppressed and exploited groups and social classes—the grassroots—and for their authentic organizations and movements.

The final aims of this combination of liberating knowledge

---

* Taken from Fals-Borda (1988), pp. 85-97. See full references in the final bibliography.

and political power within a continuous process of life and work are: (1) to enable the oppressed groups and classes to acquire sufficient creative and transforming leverage as expressed in specific projects, acts and struggles; and (2) to produce and develop sociopolitical thought processes with which popular bases can identify.

Empowering the Oppressed

In the first place, learning to interact and organize with PAR is based on the existential concept of experience proposed by the Spanish philosopher José Ortega y Gasset. Through the actual experience of something, we intuitively apprehend its essence; we feel, enjoy and understand it as reality, and we thereby place our own being in a wider, more fulfilling context. In PAR such an experience, called *vivencia* in Spanish,[2] is complemented by another idea: that of authentic commitment.

This combination of experience and commitment allows one to see for whom such knowledge is intended, in this case, the base groups themselves. Moreover, such a concept of experience recognizes that there are two types of animators or agents of change: those who are external and those who are internal to the exploited classes. Both types are unified in one sole purpose—that of achieving the shared goals of social transformation.

These animators (internal and external) contribute their own knowledge, techniques and experiences to the transformation process. But their knowledge and experience stem from different class conformations and rationalities (one Cartesian and academic, the other experiential and practical). Thus a dialectical tension is created between them which can be resolved only through practical commitment, that is, through a form of praxis. The sum of knowledge from both types of agents, however, makes it possible to acquire a much more accurate and correct picture of the reality that is being transformed. Therefore academic knowledge combined with popular knowledge and wisdom may result in total scientific knowledge of a revolutionary nature which destroys the previous unjust class monopoly.

This dialectical tension in commitment and praxis leads to a rejection of the asymmetry implicit in the subject/object relationship that characterizes traditional academic research and most tasks of daily life. According to participatory theory, such a relationship must be transformed into subject/subject rather than subject/object. Indeed, the destruction of the asymmetric binomial is the kernel of the concept of participation as understood in the present context (researcher/researched) and in other aspects of the daily routine (family, health, education, politics and so forth).

Thus to participate means to break up voluntarily and through experience the asymmetrical relationship of submission and dependence implicit in the subject/object binomial. This is the essence of participation.

The general concept of authentic participation as defined here is rooted in cultural traditions of the common people and in their real history (not the elitist version), which are resplendent with feelings and attitudes of an altruistic, cooperative and communal nature and which are genuinely democratic. They are core values that have survived from original praxis in spite of the destructive impact of conquests, violence and all kinds of foreign invasions. Such resistent values are based on mutual aid, the helping hand, the care of the sick and the old, the communal use of lands, forests and waters, the extended family, matrifocalism and many other old social practices which vary from region to region but which constitute the roots of authentic participation.

Recognition of this constructive and altruistic mode of participation, as a real and endogenous experience of and for the common people, reduces the differences between bourgeois intellectuals and grassroots communities, between elite vanguards and base groups, between experts (technocrats) and direct producers, between bureaucracies and their clients, between mental and manual labor. Hence the immense and dynamic potential for creativity that such a break-up of the subject/object binomial implies through the rejection of dogmatisms and vertical authoritarian structures, whether planned or centralized, and traditional patterns of exploitation and domination at various levels.

The collective pursuit of these goals in social, educational and political practice turns all those involved into organic intellectuals of the working classes without creating permanent hierarchies. The proof of the success of these people's intellectuals can be seen in the fact that eventually they become redundant in their places of work, that is, the transformation processes continue even without the physical presence of external agents, animators or cadres.

PAR principles on interaction and organization in praxis lead on to other important consequences, namely, that PAR induces the creation of its own field in order to extend itself in time and space, both horizontally and vertically, in communities and regions. It moves from the micro to the macro level as if in a spiral, and thus acquires a political dimension. The final evaluation or applied criterion of the methodology revolves on this political dimension and the opportunity that it offers for making theory concomitant with action.

In addition to the central ideas of culture and ethnicity, special importance is accorded to the concept of region (within the context of social formation) as a key element in the PAR interpretation of reality for the creation of inward and outward mechanisms of countervailing power. Exploitative traditional structures are thus better understood, as are the alliances of forces towards revolutionary conjunctures which may be forged under new leadership or by enlightened vanguards. Catalytic external agents play a crucial role in linking up the local dimension to regional and, at a later stage, to the national and the international levels. The particular and the general, social formation and mode of production may thus be synthesized in this manner.

In the same way, the creative sociopolitical force set in motion by PAR may also lead to the conformation of a new type of State which is less demanding, controlling and powerful, inspired by the positive core values of the people and nurtured by autochthonous cultural values based on a truly democratic and human ideal. Such a State would be neither an imitation of existing historical models, the failures of which are easy to recognize, nor a copy of earlier representative democracies. It would strive for a more even distribution of power-knowledge among its constituents, a healthier balance between State and civil society with less Leviathanic central control and more grassroots creativity and initiative, less Locke and more Kropotkin. In effect, it would seek a return to the human scale which has been lost in the recent past.

In general, PAR proposes to resolve the main contradictions of a given region through recourse to endogenous elements. By promoting these activities PAR acquires another dimension and helps clarify what "militancy" is or should be. For this reason people can be mobilized with PAR techniques from the grassroots up and from the periphery to the center so as to form social movements which struggle for participation, justice and equity without necessarily seeking to establish hierarchical political parties in the traditional mold.

These sociopolitical tasks cannot be strictly planned, generalized or copied uncritically since they imply open social systems and conjunctural processes. There are no fixed deadlines in this work, but each project persists in time and proceeds according to its own cultural vision and political expectations until the proposed goals are reached. Or it may end forthwith through impatience and/or repression.

Sociopolitical Thought Processes

In the second place, the experiences of those involved in PAR in learning to know and recognize themselves as a means of creating people's power, and the internal and external mechanisms of countervailing power, may have certain phenomenological bases.

They start with the thesis that science is not a fetish with a life of its own or something which has an absolute pure value, but is simply a valid and useful form of knowledge for specific purposes and based on relative truths. Any science as a cultural product has a specific human purpose and therefore implicitly carries those class biases and values which scientists hold as a group. It therefore favors those who produce and control it, although its unbridled growth is currently more of a threat than a benefit to humanity. For this reason it is theoretically possible that people's science may exist as an informal endogenous process (or as a more formally constructed knowledge system on its own terms). Such a character might serve as a corrective to certain destructive tendencies of the predominant forms of science, a situation in which the knowledge acquired and properly systematized serves the interests of the exploited classes. This "people's science" thus converges with the so-called "universal science."

Ideally, in such cases the grassroots and their cadres are able to participate in the research process from the very beginning, that is, from the moment it is decided what the subject of research will be. They remain involved at every step of the process until the publication of results and the various forms of returning the knowledge to the people are completed. This is a process which gives preference to qualitative rather than quantitative analysis. Its essence is the proposition that more is to be gained by using the affective logic of the heart and sentiments than the cold-headed analysis that comes from offices and laboratories. Even so, it does make use of explanatory scientific schemas of cause and effect not only in association with formal and affective logic but also dialectical logic.

With these objectives in mind, the following techniques resulting from the practice of PAR are useful in the establishment of people's countervailing power:

Collective research. This is the use of information collected and systematized on a group basis, as a source of data and objective knowledge of facts resulting from meetings, socio-dramas, public assemblies, committees, fact-finding trips and so on. This collective and dialogical method not only produces data which may be immediately corrected or verified. It also provides a social validation of objective knowledge which cannot be achieved through other individual methods based on surveys or fieldwork. In this way, confirmation is obtained of the positive values of dialogue, discussion, argumentation and consensus in the objective investigation of social realities.

Critical recovery of history. This is an effort to discover selectively, through collective memory, those elements of the past which have proved useful in the defense of the interests of exploited classes and which may be applied to the present struggles to increase conscientization. Use is thus made of popular stories and oral tradition in the form of interviews and witness accounts by older members of the community possessing good analytical memories; the search for concrete information on given periods of the past hidden in family coffers; core data "columns" and their "fleshing out"; and ideological projections, imputation, personification and other techniques designed to stimulate the collective memory.[3] In this way, folk heroes, data and facts are discovered which correct, complement or clarify official or academic accounts written with other class interests or biases in mind. Sometimes completely new and fresh information is discovered which is of major importance to regional and national history.

Valuing and applying folk culture. In order to mobilize the masses, this third technique is based upon the recognition of essential or core values among the people in each region. Account is taken of cultural and ethnic elements frequently ignored in regular political practice, such as art, music, drama, sports, beliefs, myths, story-telling and other expressions related to human sentiment, imagination and ludic or recreational tendencies.

Production and diffusion of new knowledge. This technique is integral to the research process because it is a central part of the feedback and evaluative objective of PAR. It recognizes a division of labor among and within base groups. Although PAR strives to end the monopoly of the written word, it incorporates various styles and procedures for systematizing new data and knowledge according to the level of political conscience and ability for understanding written, oral or visual messages by the base groups and public in general.

Four levels of communication are thus established, depending on whether the message and systematized knowledge are addressed to pre-literate peoples, cadres or intellectuals. A good PAR researcher should learn to address all four levels with the same message in the different styles required if he is to be really effective in the written, auditory or visual communication of the thought or message.[4]

Efficient forms of communication based on a "total" or intentional language include the use of image, sound, painting, gestures, mime, photographs, radio programs, popular theater, videotapes, audiovisual material, poetry, music, puppets and exhibitions. Finally, there are material forms of organization and economic and social action developed by base groups (cooperatives, trade unions, leagues, cultural centers, action units, workshops, training centers and so forth) as a result of the studies carried out.

There is an obligation to return this knowledge systematically to the communities and workers' organizations because they continue to be its owners. They may determine the priorities concerning its use and authorize and establish the conditions for its publication, dissemination or use. This systematic devolution of knowledge complies with the objective set by Italian socialist Antonio Gramsci of transforming "common" sense into "good" sense or critical knowledge that would be the sum of experiential and theoretical knowledge.

To succeed in these endeavors requires a shared code of com-

munication (Heller's "symmetric reciprocity" [1989: 304]) between internal elements and external agents of change which
leads to a common and mutually understandable conceptualization and categorization. The resulting plain and understandable
language is based on daily intentional expressions and is accessible to all, avoiding the airs of arrogance and the technical jargon that spring from usual academic and political practices,
including ideological elements from the current developmentalist discourse.

These PAR techniques do not exclude a flexible use of other
practices deriving from sociological and anthropological tradition, such as the open interview (avoiding any excessively rigid
structure), census or simple survey , direct systematic observation (with personal participation and selective experimentation),
field diaries, data filing, photography, cartography, statistics,
sound recording, primary and secondary source materials, and
notarial, regional and national archives. Cadres (resource persons) should not only be equipped to handle these orthodox
techniques responsibly but also know how to popularize them
by teaching the activists simpler, more economic and controllable methods of research, so that they can carry on their work
without being dependent on intellectuals or external agents and
their costly equipment and procedures.[5]

NOTES

1.   After spreading to Europe and English-speaking countries,
     PAR was the designation adopted there. "Investigación
     acción participativa" (IAP) is used in Latin America;
     "pesquisa participante" in Brazil; "ricerca partecipativa,"
     "enquête participation," "recherche action," "partizipative
     aktionsforschung" elsewhere. In our view there are no sig-
     nificant differences between these designations, especially
     between PAR and PR ("participatory research"), as can be
     observed by comparing chapters in the present book. We
     prefer to specify the action component since we want to
     make the point that "we are talking about action-research
     that is participatory, and participatory research that unites
     with action [for transforming reality]" (Rahman 1985: 108).
     Hence also our differences with other strands of action-

research, appreciative and cooperative inquiry, sociological intervention, action anthropology, etc. to which detailed reference is made in Chapter 11.

2. *Vivencia* is a Spanish neologism introduced by Ortega y Gasset when he adapted the word *Erlebnis* from German existentialist literature early in the present century. It may be translated roughly as "inner life-experience" or "happening," but the concept implies a more ample meaning by which a person finds fulfillment for his/her being, not only in the workings of the inner self but in the osmotic otherness of nature and the wider society, and by learning not with the brain alone but also with the heart. This idea has found some resonance in Jürgen Habermas' concept of the "life-world" as a totality of experience that includes daily living and concrete value contexts (Habermas 1984). *Vivencias* expressed with "the Other" incarnated in the poor are not far from the "alterity" philosophy of Emmanuel Lévinas (1974) and Tzvetan Todorov (1982) recently diffused among PAR and intellectual circles in the Third World.

3. Core data "columns" refer to hard information derived from unquestioned sources, such as dates, toponymy and concrete actors in given events which the researcher utilizes to build up his/her account before "fleshing out" the resulting structure with interpretive information, including a disciplined use of imagination. Heller (1989: 299) has recently recommended this technique, describing it as a dialectic balance between what she calls "core" and "ring" knowledge. Ideological projection is an interpretation of a past event on the basis of knowledge of present logical and cultural parameters. Imputation is the ascription to one informant, real or imaginary, of convergent, supplementary or confirmatory data obtained from different persons. Personification allows for the use of folk symbols to explain, understand or describe social trends or the ethos of a given society.

4. See, for example, my own four-volume *Historia doble de la Costa* (*Double History of the Coast*) published in Bogotá by Carlos Valencia Editores from 1979 to 1986. It is conceived and presented in two channels (one of description—mythos—and the other of systematic or theoretical discussion—logos) which run simultaneously on opposite pages.

Some critics trace this technique to novelist Julio Cortázar's *Rayuela*, although this method responds to different needs in the two works. The double channel technique appears to be spreading. Anthropologist Richard Price (1983) adopted it for presenting and discussing the culture and history of maroon tribes in Surinam, as did physicist Roland Fivaz (1989) for dealing with aesthetics in arts and sciences. It has also been used in several unpublished academic theses.

5. Especially complex or advanced technologies may be an exception, and this is carefully assessed and controlled by all parties concerned. These techniques transcend Mao Tsetung's principle of "from the masses to the masses" in that they recognize the capacity of ordinary people to systematize the data produced and recovered, that is, to participate fully in the entire research process with their own organic intellectuals from the beginning to the end, thereby avoiding continued dependence on or imposition by self-appointed vanguards. For this purpose, Habermas' recent conceptualization of the "life-world" and communicative action appears pertinent (Habermas 1984), although it applies more particularly to advanced capitalist societies. His theories of the use of language and speech acts (open and concealed), reminiscent of Mikhail Bakhtin's theory of language and utterances (Bakhtin 1986), help to establish mechanisms for reaching understanding. PAR has developed and relies on such mechanisms. We also recognize Harold Garfinkel's ethnomethological techniques of handling ordinary language and experimenting with double-voiced communication, as we do in PAR, although his claim to study invariant social phenomena in different contexts of interaction is not convincing (Garfinkel 1967).

Chapter 2

THE THEORETICAL
STANDPOINT OF PAR

Muhammad Anisur Rahman

In presenting the theoretical standpoint of participatory action-research, we may start with some elements from a statement
made in Mexico in 1982 (Rahman 1985).

The basic ideology of PAR is that a self-conscious people,
those who are currently poor and oppressed, will progressively
transform their environment by their own praxis. In this process
others may play a catalytic and supportive role but will not
dominate.

Many PAR works have been inspired by the notion of "class
struggle" as embodied in historical materialism, but PAR is opposed to certain interpretation of historical materialism that
views social transformation as primarily the task of a "vanguard"
party which assumed (itself) to have a more "advanced" consciousness relative to that of the masses. In fact, the growth of the
PAR movement in recent times seems to owe itself to the crisis
of the left as well as to the crisis of the right: vanguard parties
have produced structural change in a number of situations, but
in several of them newer forms of domination over the masses

have emerged.

The Generation of Knowledge

Such historical experience calls for rethinking on the meaning of social transformation for people's liberation. The dominant view of social transformation has been preoccupied with the need for changing the oppressive structures of relations in material production—certainly a necessary task. But, and this is the distinctive viewpoint of PAR, domination of masses by elites is rooted not only in the polarization of control over the means of material production but also over the means of knowledge production, including control over the social power to determine what is useful knowledge. Irrespective of which of these two polarizations set off a process of domination, one reinforces the other in augmenting and perpetuating this process.

By now in most polarized societies the gap between those who have social power over the process of knowledge generation, and those who have not, has reached dimensions no less formidable than the gap in access to the means of physical production. History is demonstrating that a convergence of the latter gap in no way ensures convergence of the former: on the contrary, existence of the gap in knowledge relations has been seen to offset the advantages of revolutionary closures of the gap in relations of physical production and has set off processes of domination once again.

In order to improve the possibility of liberation, therefore, these two gaps should be attacked simultaneously wherever feasible. This is not accomplished by the masses being mobilized by a vanguard body with the latter's "advanced" consciousness. People cannot be liberated by a consciousness and knowledge other than their own, and a strategy such as the above inevitably contains seeds of newer forms of domination. Consequently it is absolutely essential that the people develop their own endogenous consciousness-raising and knowledge generation, and that this process acquires the social power to assert vis-a-vis all elite consciousness and knowledge.

The generation of (scientific) knowledge does not require the method of detached observation of the positivist school. Any observation, whether it is detached or involved, its value biased, and this is not where the scientific character of knowledge is determined. The scientific character or objectivity of knowledge rests on its social verifiability, and this depends on consensus as to the method of verification. There exist different epistemological cal schools (paradigms) with different respective verification systems, and all scientific knowledge in this sense is relative to the paradigm to which it belongs and, specifically, to the verification system to which it is submitted.

In this sense the people can choose or devise their own verification system to generate scientific knowledge in their own right. An immediate objective of PAR is to return to the people the legitimacy of the knowledge they are capable of producing through their own verification systems, as fully scientific,[1] and the right to use this knowledge—including any other knowledge, but not dictated by it—as a guide in their own action. This immediate objective is an integral and indispensible part of the objective of dual social transformation—in the relations of material production and in the relations of knowledge.

People's Empowerment and Research

Since the above statement was made, PAR has been gaining increasing status among people-oriented work and agencies and is indeed being widely coopted as a methodology and a jargon without necessarily subscribing to its ideology as stated above (see Chapter 3). Another phenomenon that is happening is a deepening of both the crisis of the right and of the left.

As for the right, state leaderships are increasingly exposing themselves as oligarchies interested in plundering social wealth for personal aggrandizement, so that the very concept of the nation-state as the representative of society and helmsman of social progress is coming into question. In a number of countries, the state has come to be regarded as an entity essentially of private enterprise. On the other hand, the crisis of the left is augmented due to two factors: (1) the increasing popular questioning of the wisdom of the "vanguards," particularly in Eastern Europe; and (2) the growing evidence and admission, also at the official levels, that the promise of revolutionary development of the productive forces under socialism (as it is being institutionalized) is distant. It is becoming evident that there is a serious question whether the needed popular incentive to contribute to such development exists under socialism, while the central leaderships who have appropriated supreme power may themselves lack the needed competence, if not the motivation, to deliver such development. The deepening of both these crises is stimulating PAR activities outside the framework of the State as well as of political parties.

The growing application, status and cooptation of PAR in many quarters call for an attempt to promote greater clarity as to what it is and is not, both at the micro and the macro levels.

At the micro level, PAR is a philosophy and style of work with the people to promote people's empowerment for changing their immediate environment—social and physical—in their favor. In situations characterized by sharp class exploitation and oppression at the micro level, as observed in many countries (particularly in Asia and Latin America), this usually involves some form of class confrontation, which is often combined with collective socioeconomic initiatives to improve the short-run livelihood of the people. In situations where micro-level class exploitation is not so sharp, as in a number of African countries, people's collective action takes the form more of socioeconomic initiatives. These often confront or assert vis-a-vis those state bureaucracies and technocracies that seek to impose their ideas of "development" (modernization)—ideas which typically are alien to the people's way of life and culture and are often also destructive of the physical environment. The people's own initiatives seek to promote their authentic self-development, which takes off from their traditional culture and seeks to preserve the physical environment with which they have an organic association. Additionally, these are also often addressed to negotiating with or challenging the relevant state organs for better service in areas where they are supposed to serve.

Two elements of empowerment that are considered by PAR to be the most important are autonomous, democratic people's organizations and the restoration of the status of popular knowledge and promoting popular knowledge.

The process of autonomous organization consists of either the formation of new people's organizations if none suitable exist or the strengthening of existing popular organizations and promotion of a self-reliant, assertive culture within them. In order to promote an authentic people's movement, the process of organization is itself preceded, and thereafter accompanied, by a process of awareness-raising through a series of social inquiries by the people. These take different forms, ranging from dialogue sessions to full-scale historical and socioeconomic investigations by the people—people's research and self-knowledge generation. Transforming the relations of knowledge thus has a centrality in the entire task of empowerment.

The term "conscientization," which has been popularized by Paulo Freire (1982), is widely used to refer to raising people's awareness. As Freire has made quite clear, conscientization is a process of self-awareness-raising through collective self-inquiry and reflection. This permits exchange of information and knowledge but is opposed to any form of teaching or indoctrination. But the practice of "conscientization" often departs from this concept, and slips consciously or unconsciously into processes of knowledge transfer rather than the stimulation of and assistance to processes of the people's own inquiries to build their self-knowledge. This has nothing to do with conscientization, and in fact inhibits the development of self-awareness as well as the self-confidence needed to advance self-knowledge.

In this context the concept of establishing a subject-subject relation between the external researcher/activist and the people, as put forward in discussing PAR, needs a deeper articulation. It is not easy to establish a truly subject-subject relation at the very outset with people who are traditionally victims of a dominating structure—the inertia of traditional attitudes and images of self and of others may keep the people implicitly subordinate in a research (as well as decision-making) process in which formidable outside researcher/activists are present. And for the outside professionals also, it is not easy to avoid being carried away by their own self-images and imposing their own ideas on the people consciously or unconsciously. To counter such tendencies, it may be necessary to make the people the subject, defining the process to be one of the people's own independent inquiry, in which the outsiders may be consulted at the initiative of the people. Thus made independent and masters of themselves, the people experience their capability and power to produce knowledge autonomously. Such experience may finally clinch the matter for both sides, and a true subject-subject relation may be possible thereafter if mutual interest in a research partnership is subsequently agreed.

Therefore, while calling for a subject-subject relation between external researchers and the people, PAR views the task in a dynamic context and, depending on situations, often should go beyond the subject-subject principle to initiate the people's own research under their own control.

PAR as a Cultural Movement

So far for the function of PAR as a micro-level intervention. What is the significance of PAR for macro-level social transformation?

Typically, PAR has been initiated by so-called "voluntary" bodies, variously called "social action groups," "non-governmental organizations" or, to use a more recent nomenclature that is functionally more communicative as well as challenging, "self-reliance-promoting organizations" or SPOs (see Chapter 7).

These organizations are relatively small in scale, and do not command structures through which a national-level PAR movement could be directly initiated. PAR, however, is a growing movement in a number of countries. Possibly the largest single movement relative to national size is the Six-S movement in Burkina Faso, also noted in Chapter 7, which today has come close to covering about two-thirds of the country's villages. In Senegal the affiliates of the Federation of Non-governmental Organizations (FONGS), which subscribes to the principles of people's participation and self-reliance, have a total membership of about one million or roughly one-sixth of the country's population (although, of course, not all affiliates have attained the same standards in their work). In a number of other countries, PAR has moved beyond the village cluster level, and is a multi-district or province-level phenomenon with formal or informal structures linking the base level processes. Examples are the work of the Participatory Research Organization of Communities and Education for Self-Reliance (PROCESS) in the Philippines, covering about 280 villages and 50 towns in nine provinces, and the Organisation of Rural Associations for Progress (ORAP) which includes about 500 villages in the Matabeleland region.

Such scales of activity are being attained basically through two processes of "multiplication": (1) spontaneous spread of a movement from village to village by the demonstration of collective initiative, and by people engaged in such initiatives in one village animating and assisting such initiatives in other villages; and (2) stimulation of such processes in other areas by the agency (SPO) which initiated the work in some areas to start with. This has required new recruitments in this agency to do field "animation" work,[2] and/or a "phasing out" of field workers from older areas where people's organizations progressively become independent of external animation work, thus releasing workers in the SPO for initiating such processes in newer areas. New SPOs may also enter into the scene to initiate PAR in other areas.

How far such multiplication processes may move in any given country and at what speed cannot be predicted, just as it cannot be predicted how far any other effort for social transformation, "revolutionary" or otherwise, may spread in any country where such effort has to move through significant resistance and also needs qualified manpower of its own to expand in scale. However, in terms of macro-social transformation, PAR at this stage may be viewed more as a cultural movement, independent of (in some countries in link with) political movements for people's liberation rather than a political alternative itself. The need for such a cultural movement arises from the growing crises of the left referred to above, and in particular from the failure of revolutionary vanguards of the orthodox order to deliver, with their assumed "advanced consciousness," social transformation that truly promotes people's liberation.

Leadership and Consciousness

The claim of "advanced consciousness" is, in fact, a false one. Consciousness is derived from realities that people live (social existence),[3] and people living entirely different realities develop consciousnesses which are not comparable within the same scale of assessment. Even at a very mechanical level, a professional intellectual would certainly know a lot which a factory worker or a peasant might not know, but the converse is true also. Besides, it may be suggested that professional research is still rather "primitive" in its understanding (and in knowing how to understand) the complex forces—social, cultural, ethnic, psychological—which influence the course of an attempted social transformation.[4] But beyond this mechanical research question, truth (knowledge), as discussed in the 1982 statement referred to at the beginning of this chapter, is relative. It is in fact an organic part of one's social existence which generates its own paradigm for the discovery of truth (implicit or explicit science). And the people's truth in this sense is different, not backward or advanced (except in terms of its own endogenous evolution only) in relation to the truth which the professional/political activist can ever discover by his/her observation of the people's reality. The two truths may only dialogue with each other, but none may claim to be the greater of the two.

The fact, nevertheless, that movements seeking macro-social transformations have been led in general by persons coming from the professional-intellectual tradition is explained not by the intellectual superiority of these persons but by the fact that such persons by their social and economic status have in general been in a more privileged position to provide this leadership, irrespective of the value of their intellect. The working class is engaged in a daily struggle for livelihood, or in any case is constrained in employment situations from which it is far more difficult to provide the macro-level political leadership that would require the spending of paid time and mobility not easy for members of this class to arrange. The fact that political leadership of movements for emancipation of the people becomes concentrated in the hands of intellectuals is, therefore, by itself no evidence of the relative levels of understanding of the questions that are involved. There are examples of the ordinary people pronouncing profound wisdoms as well as of the highly educated pronouncing profound nonsense.

While self-emancipation of the "working class" was, indeed, the original revolutionary vision of Marx and Engels (Draper 1977), it may be suggested that the situational difficulty of the working class initiating its own liberation on a macro scale creates a vacuum in leadership which gets filled in by intellectual-activists trained in the schools rather than in life. It is a tragedy of the first order that these very intellectuals in their great wisdom not only fail to recognize the limitations of their knowledge and understanding. They also do not recognize the alienation between themselves and the people, overlooking or denying the new dialectics they introduce in the social scene by assuming revolutionary leadership even if this were fully well intentioned.

In essence, what have been overlooked or denied are the negative forces that are generated by the very fact of a social revolution and reconstruction led and managed by professional "vanguards." Some of these negative forces follow.

First, the assumption of superiority of consciousness often explicit in such initiatives inflates the ego and invites attempts to perpetuate power in "honest" conviction. Since this conviction, as we have discussed, is not validatable through scientific reasoning—the two consciousnesses in question being rooted in different social existences—it is also prone to provoke a psychologically defensive response if questioned, and this is liable to harden the tendency to dictate.

Second, assuming that revolutionaries are often very committed persons when they start their courageous pursuits, commitment itself is subject to transformation with the evolution of one's social existence. It often collapses from defeat, but may also diffuse or degenerate through the attainment of success that brings glory and power, altogether new experiences in one's existence. And commitment has also sometimes shown its fragility in the face of attractive temptations.

Third, a progressively successful political movement, as it grows in size and space and approaches a real possibility of the "final victory," attracts elements not necessarily identical to the commitment of the movement's initiators. The newcomers respond to a different historical condition altogether. The expanding scale of the movement and its new responsibilities also necessitates the enlisting of diverse forces as a part of, or as allies of, the movement, the private interests of which may also be very different from the commitment of the movement itself. And forces opposed to the movement also seek to take over, coopt or infiltrate it as it threatens to become, or actually becomes, successful.

Finally, structures and institutions which are created to dictate over the people, albeit with a "commitment," are dangerous tools as they can be taken over by anti-commitment. In any case, there is no assured method of transferring commitment to succeeding generations who have not lived through the struggles from which commitment is socio-historically born. And then the structure, if it is not accountable to the people, becomes a happy hunting ground for self-seekers. And genuine accountability to the people is not merely a matter of formal institutional structures but also, and critically, of people's self-awareness and the promotion of this awareness, and the confidence to assert their self-awareness as their political statement in the affairs of the society. Only then can there be an environment of real democracy—a relation of dialogue between social elements, all of whom have to be treated as equals.

Democracy, in any case, is a necessity for a revolutionary development of the productive forces—democracy that gives a truly productive class (or classes) the freedom to take initiatives. Capitalism cannot thrive without a form of democracy in which the capitalist class is free to venture. Unfortunately, so-called "socialist democracy" has often, in theory as well as in practice, bypassed this maxim, and the essential notion of freedom of the working class (including the peasantry) to take creative initiatives has been substituted by bureaucratic planning and a lack of initiative. Bureaucracies, whether administrative or political, are not a productive class and are typically conservative and non-enterprising. There cannot be revolutionary development of the productive forces with the "initiative" resting in a non-productive class. The crisis of the left—and for that matter, the crisis of the right as well—ultimately boils down to this dissociation between the productive forces and the leadership of concerned societies.

With such dissociation prevailing in any society, the need is to generate social processes which would promote the possibility of an organic leadership ("organic vanguard") to emerge—a leadership which would organically, and not merely intellectually, belong to and represent the interests of significant productive forces in the society. PAR, recognizing the working people as a truly productive class whose initiatives are being thwarted by the domination of non-productive forces, is an attempt to generate such processes. It is admittedly a modest attempt so far in most countries where it has been initiated, with no immediate promise at the macro-level. But most macro-level promises, in any case, have been demonstrated to be false promises.

It is, however, at least possible that from out of the culture of PAR may emerge elements that would give a better balance in the macro scene benefiting the initiatives of the people. Leaders may emerge to become a part of macro social-transformative efforts and thereby influence their course of progress; the culture of PAR may set a standard for working with the people and challenge macro vanguards to demonstrate their commitment; the deepening of popular awareness, if PAR is successful, may work as a countervailing force against attempts at domination; and the social formations (aware and assertive people's organizations and popular movements) promoted by PAR may be expected to support the best macro leadership that exists or that may emerge in the society.

While these are hopeful speculations about the macro significance of PAR, the need for permanent vigilance and self-criticism exists for the PAR movement itself. Apart from the cooptation which is taking place, the instability of commitment discussed above applies to PAR as much as to the more conventional trends in social activism. This is true, of course, also of people's own leaders. In the face of such instability—and this is the ultimate test of anyone's commitment—it is imperative to recognize and admit this possibility of degeneration, and initiate popular analysis of this phenomenon as an essential element of people's self-awareness, so that this possibility is known to all and illusions to the contrary are discouraged. As Nyoni has observed in Chapter 8, the very notion of participation implies that nothing should be hidden from the people. PAR has the best chance of surviving the test of time only if it tells the people that it can betray them, and that only an aware and ever-vigilant people is not betrayed.

NOTES

1. One may distinguish between popular knowledge, which has been consciously and systematically generated by a process of collective inquiry ("explicit science"), and that which has been generated spontaneously but is widely shared ("implicit science").
2. In PAR activities, "animation" is broadly defined to be the stimulation of people's self-inquiry, self-image and self-action. For a discussion of the term, see Tilakaratna (1987).
3. Cf. Karl Marx, *Theses on Feuerbach.* (See end bibliography.)
4. For example, the tenacity or resilience of religious and ethnic consciousness in post-revolutionary societies was hardly anticipated by the orthodox left, and they do not seem to have any tools to grapple with such dimensions of social reality until now.

Chapter 3

A SELF-REVIEW OF PAR

Muhammad Anisur Rahman and Orlando Fals-Borda

Almost twenty years have passed since the first attempts were made in Third World countries at participatory action-research. Two opposite trends took place as the idea spread through sociopolitical structures: one toward empowerment of grassroots peoples; the other, largely unanticipated by the originators, reached out to the elites and dominant groups with an electrifying effect.

Stages and Points of Departure

Those of us who had the privilege in the late 1960s of taking part in this cultural, political and scientific *vivencia* tried to respond to the dismal situation of our societies, the over-specialization and emptiness of academic life and the sectarian practices of much of the revolutionary left. We felt that radical transformations were necessary and urgent in society and in the use of scientific knowledge, which generally in our societies lagged behind in the Newtonian age with its reductionist, instrumental orientations. As a starter, we decided to look for adequate answers by devoting ourselves to the plight of those who had been victimized by the oligarchies and their "development" policies: the poor communities in rural areas.

Our initial work until 1977 was characterized by an activist and somewhat anti-professional bent (many of us quit university posts); hence the importance given to such innovative field research techniques as "social intervention" as well as "militant research" with a political party organization in mind. We also applied "concientization" as well as "commitment" and "insertion" in the social process. Among us, some found inspiration in certain Gandhian strands, others in the classic Talmudian Marxism then in vogue—or in both. And some were driven by humanist urges of their own. Our personal moods and loyalties strongly rejected such established institutions as governments, traditional political parties, churches and academia in such a way that those years can be seen mostly as an iconoclastic period. Yet certain constants began to appear that would accompany us throughout subsequent periods up to today, such as the emphasis on holistic viewpoints and qualitative methods of analysis.

Early activism and radicalism gave way to reflection without losing our impulse in the field. This search for balance was displayed in the World Symposium on Action-Research and Scientific Analysis held in Cartagena, Colombia, in March 1977 and organized by Colombian institutions and other national and international bodies. One theoretical father figure besides Marx became prominent in that event and in later similar occasions: Antonio Gramsci. We also revised traditional and current notions of "participation."

During this self-assessment or reflective stage, we discovered and insisted upon clarity in theoretical propositions, such as on participation, democracy and pluralism. These theses gave orientation to our subsequent work. We started to understand PAR not merely as a methodology of research with the subject/subject relationship evolving in symmetrical, horizontal or non-exploitative patterns in social, economic and political life. We saw it also as a part of social activism with an ideological and spiritual commitment to promote people's (collective) praxis. Of course, this also turned out to be that of the activists (PAR researchers) at the same time, since the life of everybody is—formally or informally—some kind of praxis. But the promotion of people's collectives and their systematic praxis became, and has continued to be, a primary objective of PAR.

Translation of such ideas into practice—and vice-versa, sometimes with divergent views—became the task of several colleagues in many parts of the world. Besides those co-authoring the present book, they include the Bhoomi Sena group in India; the late Andrew Pearse in Colombia/England and Anton de Schutter in Mexico/Holland; Gustavo Esteva, Rodolfo Stavenhagen, Ricardo Pozas, Salvador Garcia, Martin de la Rosa, Lourdes Arizpe and Luis Lópezllera in Mexico; Walter Fernandes, Rajesh Tandon,D. L. Sheth and Dutta Savle in India; Majid Rahnema, Kemal Mustafa, Wilbert Tengay and Francis Mulwa in Africa; Marja Liisa Swantz in Finland; Cynthia Nelson in Egypt; Guy LeBoterf in Nicaragua/France; João Bosco Pinto, João Francisco de Souza, Carlos Rodrígues Brandão and Michel Thiollent in Brazil; Ernesto Parra, Alvaro Velasco, John Jairo Cárdenas, Victor Negrete, Augusto Libreros, Guillermo Hoyos and Leon Zamosc in Colombia; Harald Swedner and Anders Rudqvist in Sweden; Xavier Albo' and Silvia Rivera in Bolivia; Heinz Moser and Helmut Ornauer in Germany and Austria; Budd Hall and Ted Jackson in Canada; Mary Racelis in the Philippines; Jan de Vries and Thord Erasmie in Holland; D.E. Comstock and Peter Park in the United States; Stephen Kemmis and Robin McTaggart in Australia; Francisco Vio Grossi in Chile; Ricardo Cetrulo in Uruguay; Oscar Jara, Carlos Nuñez, Raul Leis, Felix Cadena, Malena de Montis, Francisco Lacayo in Central America, and many others. (References to the contributions of many of these PAR researchers are found in the bibliographical section at the end of this book.) Some institutions like the International Labour Office (Employment and Development Department), the United Nations Research Institute for Social Development, the International (ICAE) and Latin American (CEAAL) Councils for Adult Education, the Society for International Development (with Ponna Wignaraja) and the United Nations University in Asia furnished inputs to our movement.

With a first formal presentation of our subject in academic circles in 1982 during the 10th World Congress of Sociology in Mexico City (Rahman 1985), and as a result of the previous reflective stage and the impact of real-life processes, PAR achieved more self-identity and advanced from micro, peasant and local community issues to complex, urban, economic and regional dimensions. Especially prominent were the expectations of grassroots independent political and civic movements (seldom established political parties) that wanted theoretical and systematic support from us in our countries.

PAR researchers proceeded then to employ the comparative approach—in Nicaragua, Mexico, and Colombia (Fals-Borda 1988)—and to expand it to such fields as medicine and public health, ("barefoot") economics, planning, history, (liberation) theology, (post-ontological) philosophy, anthropology, (non-positivist) sociology and social work. Awareness increased on the importance of considering knowledge as power, learning to interchange information in workshops and seminars and the need to train a new type of social activist. Attempts at international coordination among ourselves were made in several places (Santiago de Chile, Mexico, New Delhi, Colombo, Dar-es-Salaam, Rome), and an International Group for Grass-Roots Initiatives (IGGRI) was launched in 1986. There was a quiet decantation of ideas and practices during the last years, including an epistemological discussion on linkages and ends, in what appeared to be an expansive period.

PAR showed further signs of intellectual and practical maturity as encouraging information arrived from fieldwork and through publications in several languages on unquestionable achievements in the recovery of landed estates (alas, often bloody), in public health practices combined with folk medicine, in popular education; in attempting technological adoption controls among peasants; and in stimulating women's liberation, supportive popular theater and protest music, Christian-oriented communities and so on.

This evidence naturally proved to be tempting as an alternative for those agencies that for decades had been doing parallel "development work," especially in community development, cooperativism, vocational and adult education and agricultural extension, without convincing results. Thus formerly sceptic or contemptuous eyes were increasingly turned to PAR experiences. Criticism of "dualism," "modernization" and "development" ideologies grew. There was more tolerance and understanding, and the gate was open for cooptation gestures by the "Establishment" as well as for convergence with colleagues sympathetic with our postulates but who had taken different points of departure. As our approach gained respectability, many officials and researchers began to claim that they were working with PAR when in actuality they were doing something quite different. This challenged us to sharpen the conceptions so that there was no confusion, to develop defense responses against cooptation and to dilute manipulation by established institutions. Of course, cooptation appears to be a natural process since it has affected any worthwhile principle of social life, such as democracy, cooperation and socialism, and is in fact a measure of the popular appeal of such principles.

Awareness of Cooptation

Symptoms of PAR cooptation are evident. For example, many universities—among them California, Calgary, Massachusetts, Nacional de Colombia, Hohenheim, Puerto Rico and Helsinki—have offered or are offering seminars and workshops on participatory research as a substitute for "applied science" courses. A number of colleagues have resumed academic careers, including one of the present co-editors. Prestigious professional journals have published pertinent articles (for example, Fals-Borda 1987 in *International Sociology,* and Rahman 1987a in *Evaluation Studies Review Annual,* on applied psychologists who thus discover the "inherently conservative nature of [present] program evaluation"). The last international congresses of sociology, rural sociology, anthropology, social work and Americanists have included well-attended PAR discussions and forums. Many governments have appointed participatory researchers and allowed for in-house experimentation in this regard. United Nations agencies have recognized PAR as a viable alternative, even though it challenges their established traditions of "delivery systems," "consultants" and "experts." And non-governmental organizations are looking through participatory approaches for ways to more decisive group action, to transform themselves into truly grassroots supporting groups and to overcome the paternalist and dependency-fostering practices that have been hampering their work. These entities have eased the transition by using adjectives like "integrated," "participatory," and "sustainable" or "self-fulfilling" to describe development.

Of course, not everything these institutions call participatory is authentic according to our ontological definition, and much confusion has been sown in this regard. So we always try to emphasize PAR's particular philosophy and practical results in order to counter such faulty assimilation. In this respect, the opinion of real communities involved, taken as "reference groups" with their own verification system, is of paramount importance. Results are seen in real life, thus evaluations can be performed apart from mere internal consistency rules or statistical criteria. As utilization of authentic PAR on a grand scale and of the principles of countervailing people's power often invites repression by vested interests and governments, this is still another symptom to watch.

It is important to be conscious of the fact that the described cooptation process is now full-fledged. Theoretical and methodological convergence with PAR has also advanced, sometimes without complete realization of the merger of conceptions and procedures (see Chapter 11). These signs have multiple consequences for PAR. Leaving aside justifiable claims of victory over certain dominant systems of thought and policy, there are dangers for the survival of original PAR ideals, even certain feelings of betrayal. But there is also a healthy compulsion to modify our present vision and mission of PAR as we place it in a wider historical perspective and look beyond it.

We hope that the present book will serve to examine these trends constructively in such a way that we can at least walk into the future, underscoring our primary intent and reviving our critical concerns. We should have no regrets over our original iconoclasm.[1] And it is well to remind ourselves and others at this challenging moment that a rather permanent existential choice is made when one decides to live and work with PAR. Our proposal has not been, nor is now, a finished product, an easy blueprint or a panacea. We should recall that PAR, while emphasizing a rigorous search for knowledge, is an open-ended process of life and work—or *vivencia*—a progressive evolution toward an overall, structural transformation of society and culture, a process that requires ever renewed commitment, an ethical stand, self-critique and persistence at all levels. In short, it is a philosophy of life as much as a method.

This philosophical, ethical and methodological choice is a permanent task. Moreover, it should be made more general: a committed PAR researcher/activist would not want to help those oligarchical classes that have accumulated capital, power and knowledge thus far and so recklessly. These classes themselves know that they have mismanaged such resources for society, culture and nature by advocating and inventing exploitative and oppressive structures.

Therefore what appears clearly at issue for PAR now and in the future is increasing the input and control of enlightened common people—the subordinate classes, the poor, the peripheral, the voiceless, the untrained, the exploited grassroots in general—over the process of production of knowledge and its storage and its use. One purpose is to break up and/or transform the present power monopoly of science and culture exercised by elitist, oppressive groups (Rahman 1985: 119; cf. Hall 1978).[2] Another purpose is to continue to stimulate and support people's movements for progress and socioeconomic justice, and to facilitate their transition into the political arena (Fals-Borda 1989).

The Present Significance of PAR

Is PAR needed today in our societies as much as it appeared to us to be twenty years ago? Within the limitations of all natural processes and known social movements that undergo the birth-élan-death cycle, the answer is Yes, provided we also see PAR as a bridge toward more satisfying forms of explanation of realities and of action to transform those realities. We should be looking beyond PAR since the present cooptation-convergence stage is bound to lead us onto something else that would be qualitatively different and hopefully as useful and significant for the achievement of the original purposes of PAR. We do not know still what it will be, perhaps an enriched, creative PAR. We have to wait and see in order to activate the growth of the chrysalis that would come out of the PAR cocoon as it now is.

With this proviso, it may be said now that perhaps there are more arguments in favor of a continued utilization of PAR today than was the case in 1970. As Walter Benjamin once wrote, there is a wish that the planet will one day sustain a civilization that has abandoned blood and horror. We feel that PAR as a heuristic research procedure and altruistic way of life may continue and abet that wish.

In general, it is clear that the world is still passing through the same era of confusion and conflict in which PAR was born. A number of countries characterized by class oppression hold large sections of the population deprived of productive assets, turning people into dependent beings. This produces material suffering, human indignity, a loss of strength to assert one's voice or culture—in short, a loss of self-determination. There is a degeneration of political democracy to, at best, periodic balloting to choose persons from among the privileged to rule over the underprivileged, thus perpetuating class oppression. Such is the case in most countries termed democratic, advanced or developed. But similar signs can be observed in socialist countries where elites also have failed to deliver sustained improvement to the material and cultural lives of the people, not to mention their betrayal of the socialist promise of working people empowered to create their own history.

Participatory action-research has allowed us to study and act upon this tragic situation in terms of knowledge relations that go beyond the ritual of analyzing processes and structures of material production. This may help us in justifying the persistence of our approach. As recalled, we can see that a key weapon in the hands of the elites to make the people wait upon them for leadership and initiative, whether for "development" or for social change, has been the assumed superiority of formal knowledge. Of this type of knowledge, the elites have a monopoly, unlike popular knowledge.

Self-proclaimed vanguards have used this monopoly to assert their credentials in leading people toward revolutionary mobilization as well as toward post-revolutionary reconstruction. Leaders in other societies with their own educational credentials and with an array of professionals serving them, shared a similar presumption.

Unequal relations of knowledge are therefore a critical factor that perpetuates class or elite domination over the people. They reproduce new forms of domination if old forms are eliminated without care and prevision. We claim that PAR can continue to be a world movement toward the improvement of this condition by stimulating popular knowledge—knowledge existing as local or indigenous science and wisdom, to be advanced by the people's self-inquiry—as a principal basis for popular action for social and political change and for genuine progress in achieving equality and democracy.

As part of this scientific and political task, we have hoped that PAR would work "beyond development" and beyond itself toward a cultural awakening and toward a humanistic reorientation of Cartesian technology and instrumental rationality through stressing the importance of the human scale and the qualitative as well as by demythifying research and its technical jargon (see Feyerabend 1987). Likewise, we have tried to work simultaneously so that popular wisdom and common sense are enriched and defended for the necessary advancement of the poor and exploited in a more just, productive and democratic type of society. Our interest has been to try to combine both knowledges, so that appropriate procedures can be invented or adopted without killing particular cultural roots. In a similar manner these procedures should give the common people—as the very subject of history—greater leverage and control over the process of knowledge generation.

This remains an essential task for us and for many others, one in which the best and most constructive academic knowledge could be subsumed with pertinent and congruent folk science. PAR activists have been building "reenchantment bridges" between both traditions. It appears important to persevere in this work in order to produce a science that truly liberates, a knowledge for life.

Finally, there remains the matter of the problematic nature of present state power with its violent leanings and expressions. We have become used to viewing the authoritarian, centralized nation-state as something given or natural, as a fetish. Indeed, much energy of several generations has been spent in building such political machines and power structures since the sixteenth century, with known unsatisfactory results. Today PAR practitioners and many others are seeing the need to reverse this tide and to give civil society another opportunity again—a chance to recharge and exercise its diffused strength. This is people's countervailing power, an effort from the bottom up and from the periphery to the centers, that would halt the unconditional feeding of the derivative power of the Prince (witness what happened recently with dramatic results in Eastern Europe, Brazil, Chile, Mexico, Haiti and the Philippines). Hence the present trends toward autonomy, self-reliance and decentralization; the rise of regions and provinces; and the reorganization of obsolete national structures pursued by many grassroot, cultural, ethnic, social and political newer movements and entities throughout the world—a number of which have been connected with or nurtured by PAR.

Much of our contemporary world has been constructed on

the basis of hate, greed, intolerance, chauvinism, dogmatism, autism and conflict. PAR philosophy would propose to stimulate the dialectical opposites of those attitudes. If the initial subject/object binomial is to be solved in horizontal dialogics and in "the one subject," as claimed by PAR, this process would have to affirm the importance of "the Other" and become heterologous. To respect differences, to hear discrete voices, to recognize the right of fellow human beings to act, live and let live, to feel the "exotopian," as Mikhail Bakhtin (1986) would say, may turn into a strategic characteristic of our time. When we discover ourselves in others, we affirm our own personality and culture and attune ourselves to a vivified cosmos.

These destructive/constructive, yin-yang and pluralistic ideals appear to be related to deep popular sentiments for security and peace with justice, in defense of multiple and cherished ways of life and for resistance against homogenization. They are fed by a return to nature in its diversity, a survival reaction to those patterns of dominance (mostly male) that have left the world half-destroyed, culturally less rich and threatened by lethal forces.

If PAR can facilitate these tasks so that freedom is gained without wrath, and enlightenment with transparency, it may be clear that PAR's continuity and function in tying up with subsequent evolutive stages—in practice and in theory—are plainly justified. This book is one more token of the same old commitment.

Other reasons could be adduced to see that participatory action-research may still have a role to play for today and tomorrow. But it is better if we let the co-authors of this book speak for themselves. They express their own *vivencias*, each one in his/her own way, looking at very fresh and recent experiences on knowledge use and power abuse through their own cultural glasses (why not?), and deducing lessons, methods, concepts and theories that may be of wide utility: Gianotten and de Wit among the mountain peasantry of Ayacucho in Peru; Salazar breaking authority structures with child laborers in the city of Bogotá; de Roux in conjunction with a black community in Cauca against an irrational computer; the colleagues who provided glimpses of the "other Africa"; Nyoni sharing insights on elements of people's power in Zimbabwe; Gaventa describing participatory approaches to "knowledge democracy" in North

America; plus some ground-breaking theoretical and practical reflections on sensitization of animators in South and Southeast Asia by Tilakaratna. None of us would claim that we are discovering universal or permanent truths or laws. We believe we have advanced that much beyond Newton with PAR and other intellectual and scientific pursuits. But while approaching today's realities—quite often painful—we still would want to learn new lessons in the hope of a better future for humankind.

NOTES

1. It is interesting to recall René Descartes' initial troubles at the University of Leiden when he proposed his method, wrote it in French (not in Latin) as a challenge to academia and then quit his position under charges of being an Anabaptist. What the victorious Cartesians did later with the method is another subject, equally pertinent to us.

2. We want this book to be also a step in this anti-monopolistic direction. Even though it is framed in intellectual terms so as to stimulate a dialogue between activists and scholars, we have identified ways to reach our peoples as soon as possible with these ideas and messages in their own languages, and without unnecessary impediments to their understanding, following our methodology of communication and popular education.

    We hope, therefore, that our book will be both a practical stimulus to social change through participatory action and a contribution to the growing literature on PAR, furthering its conceptual development. Another important recent addition to this literature is William Foote Whyte's new book, *Participatory Action Research* (London: Sage Publications, 1991), although he and most of his co-authors do not acknowledge the original Third World work on PAR. The editors of the present book note Whyte's contribution to our field, especially his analysis of the Mondragón cooperative experience in Spain (1988), which he now classifies as PAR.

Part II

VIVENCIAS

Chapter 4

TOGETHER AGAINST THE COMPUTER: PAR AND THE STRUGGLE OF AFRO-COLOMBIANS FOR PUBLIC SERVICES

Gustavo I. de Roux

The following account describes an experience in participatory action-research that was undertaken by Afro-Colombian communities at the southern end of the Cauca river valley in Colombia, with the cooperation of outside agents from two "self-reliance promoting organizations"—Empresa de Cooperación al Desarrollo (EMCODES) and Fundación El Palenque—interested in promoting popular education and strengthening grassroots organizations. This essay is limited to describing the ways in which information to support a collective bargaining effort was gathered and organized, and strategies for action developed by community organizations known as Public Service Users Committees (Comités de Usuarios de Servicios

Públicos) to improve their negotiating ability with the state electric company that operated in the area. Other grassroots organizations in the region have had similar experiences related to other issues; they have defended their interests, changed situations that adversely affected them and reaffirmed their role in the effort to effect social change.

It should be noted that knowledge itself was not the main motivation for carrying out the research project; rather, the main aim was to breathe new life into a struggle that had been waged since the region was first electrified. That is, the knowledge acquired was important primarily insofar as it led to new insights that were brought to bear in the struggle to transform the prevailing social conditions. As is often the case with grassroots organization's efforts linked to social dynamics and popular expectations, the urge to learn about the problem stemmed from the people's indignation and discontent, which in this case had to do with obvious irregularities in the administration of the local electricity service. That indignation led to a predisposition to take action. In other words, the research topic and its timeline were determined by the people's day-to-day pace of life, concrete interests and the importance they attributed to taking the initiative to change their living conditions. Also, as is generally the case in such experiences, the research initiative had to be carried out amid the vicissitudes of the community's pace of life, which did not come to a halt to accommodate the research.

This makes it difficult to say exactly when the research began. Being generous, it could be said that the people, observing their reality on an ongoing basis and from their cultural frames of reference, interpreting it, drawing conclusions and taking action to change it, do not let themselves get caught up in rigid temporal perspectives. Such a process does not necessarily require outside researchers to become a participatory action-research initiative. Unfortunately, the shroud of academic mystification has meant that often research is considered possible only when legitimized from outside, or when it is formally dubbed "research." This is probably due to the value ascribed in academia to well-organized information that endeavors to explain reality through the written word, an art usually reserved for intellectuals. But knowledge that is generated by people in their daily struggle to survive is not codified and transcribed in articles or books, but in folk sayings and other popular expressions as they add to their cultural baggage. That is why it is difficult for the academic community to recognize such a process as research.

The research initiative described here did not begin at a precise moment in time, insofar as it was a procedure for strengthening a process that was already underway, with a dynamic of its own and its own ups and downs. But trying to be rigorous, and for the sake of placing it in a time frame, it could be said that the research per se began when residents of Villarrica, organizing a group they called the Public Users Committee, decided to collectively plan and carry out actions to solve the electricity problem. That decision meant having to reflect on the problem and jointly reviewing the results of the actions they carried out. The decision was made in early 1981, but the most dynamic moments in this experience occurred between 1985 and 1988.

The Regional Context

Villarrica is a community of some 9,000 inhabitants, located in the southern Cauca river valley in southwestern Colombia. Like neighboring communities, it is populated primarily by Afro-Colombians, descendants of slaves brought to the region mainly in the seventeenth and eighteenth centuries to work as laborers on haciendas and in gold mines.

The 100,000 hectares of land at the southern end of the valley, which had been concentrated in a few large haciendas, operated until the mid-nineteenth century on the basis of slave labor. The oral history of the region is replete with episodes of rebellion, specially of *cimarrones* (Maroons) who, fleeing from forced labor and making their way past the foremen who supposedly watched over them, took refuge in the forests of the same haciendas, forging their own forms of survival. After the 1851 abolition of slavery in Colombia, former slaves transformed the hacienda forests into family farms which they claimed for themselves.

When the last declared civil war in Colombia (1899 to 1902) came to an end, the landowners of the region enlisted the help of the authorities to try to expel the blacks from the occupied lands by brute force. The peasants resisted, defending themselves against evictions and upholding their right to keep the farms they had been working for several decades. This process gave rise to an economically and socially autonomous black peasantry, made up of small- and medium-scale landowners, whose lands were for the most part planted with cacao trees. Around 1940 the black peasants, responsible for the region's prosperity, ethnic self-affirmation and cultural identity, accounted for some 40 percent of all cacao produced in Colombia.

Beginning in 1960, when the U.S. economic blockage against Cuba led to an increase in Colombia's sugar exports to the United States, the sugar entrepreneurs, motivated by an expanded market, extended cane production to the southern end of the valley and thereby entered into competition with the black peasants for land and labor. Promoted by the prospect of receiving high prices for their lands, and subjected to extra-economic pressures that often included violence, many peasants were forced to sell their lands. Communities such as Villarrica, which thirty years ago were marketplaces for peasant products, became marketplaces for a labor force drawn from farmer wage earners whose real incomes have been gradually shrinking. Expansion of the sugar economy brought to the region both agricultural development and rural underdevelopment, growth of the gross regional product and a decreasing standard of living, and prosperity for the few and impoverishment for the majority.

The runaway slaves' struggles for freedom, and their peasant descendants' struggles for land, find continuity in the present-day population's efforts to reaffirm their autonomy by articulating their own thinking—concepts rooted in their history—as a frame of reference for new organizational forms that uphold their right to public service and defend their communities from monopoly capital. The last two decades have witnessed land struggles, civic and popular movements, strikes for better wages, land invasions to build housing, attempts to win greater representation (as blacks) in the municipal governments and even efforts to defend the right to a clean environment. Mobilization of the region's communities, supported by the participatory action-research initiative described here, unfolded in this context.

The Electricity Problem and the Need for Research

The community of Villarrica has had problems with the

electric service, practically since it was installed in the early 1960s. At first the people tolerated the shortcomings, figuring that after all they had benefitted from access to electric lighting. But little by little, and as electricity became increasingly important to their daily lives and essential to small businesses, individual members of the community began to complain from time to time about the poor quality of the service. The first massive protests in Villarrica in the early 1970s were geared mainly toward improved electric service; at the time, there were power outages "every time it rained" due to defective power lines and lack of sufficient transformers. In 1972 an engineer from the electric company was detained until service was restored after an extended interruption due to defects in the high voltage lines. There were sporadic protests throughout the 1970s to demand that something be done about electricity supply problems. The most insistent demands were for quality and continuity in the service.

The availability of electricity created new needs. People had begun purchasing home appliances, taking advantage of what appeared to be good deals at commercial outlets in relatively nearby cities—Cali, Santander, Jamundi and Puerto Tejada. These stores sent salesmen door-to-door to promote sales of household goods on credit, quite alluring in low-income communities. Many woodstoves were replaced by electric stoves, among other reasons because it was much harder to obtain firewood for fuel as sugar cane cultivation spread. Refrigerators, irons and television sets also began to appear, all of which led to a rapid increase in per capita electricity consumption; there were also bills to pay resulting from the purchase of appliances.

In the early 1980s the international economic crisis, relating to the foreign debt burden and the subsequent need to make debt service payments, pressured the state institutions (especially in the energy sector) to adjust their rate schedules upward, thus forcing the consumers to bear the burden of fulfilling the country's commitments to the international banking community. Low-income communities where most incomes were spent meeting such basic needs as food were the hardest hit, and inhabitants faced the possibility of having to halt or drastically reduce their electricity consumptions, which by then had become a daily need.

The situation was dramatic in many small communities of

the region because the electric company, as a result of the crisis, also stopped underwriting the cost of installing power lines and transformers. Thus the inhabitants of these communities had to assume the overall cost of installation, including putting up power lines over distances of five kilometers or more. The Agrarian Bank (Caja de Crédito Agrario) agreed to extend loans to the peasants so that they would be able to assume these costs. Purchasing equipment with borrowed capital led to being faced with loan amortization and interest payments, all of which added to the already high cost of electricity. If to this we also add the debts that many semi-proletarian peasants already had incurred with the Agrarian Bank for production loans for farms affected by the expansion of the sugar cane plantations, we see a clearly risky and indeed dangerous situation. The peasants could have easily found themselves forced to sell off their lands at an accelerated pace.

Concurrent with these difficulties, people also began to notice that their monthly electric statements included many irregularities. First, they showed month-to-month changes in consumption figures that in many cases could not have been real. Also, similar consumption totals were being charged at different rates per kilowatt-hour. Finally, in some communities people noted that the bills were higher in June and December when the company had to pay employee benefits.

Individual complaints began to proliferate. They were communicated to a company official based in the area, who took charge of passing them on to the main office in the departmental capital, Popayan. In some isolated cases the claims were accepted, but in most cases the company simply accumulated the debt when it was not paid, threatened to cut off service and charged interest on the amount each user accumulated. On one occasion when several people went together to the main office to speak with the engineer in charge of their area, he answered that the calculations were done on a computer and that "the computer does not make mistakes."

Convinced that however distinguished and respectable the "computer," it was erring in the company's favor and doing consumers a disservice—and that efforts and pressures brought to bear up to that moment had only resulted in minimal changes in the company's practices—a group of approximately twenty people, mostly women, decided to form a Public Service Users

Committee. As such, they would lead the struggle for the right to quality electric service at reasonable and consistent rates. They added several variations to the previous years' demands: an end to irregularities in billing, cancellation of accumulated debts and the right to electricity at prices in line with the population's means.

The Committee felt the people had to strengthen their negotiating capacity. Two things were needed. First, evidence in support of the people's points of view had to be gathered and organized into sufficiently tight arguments to defeat the computer. That is, more research had to be done on the electricity problem to discover its roots and determine how it was manifested in specific cases. In other words, a more comprehensive understanding of the situation and its causes was needed, as were solid, watertight arguments. Second, community participation and organization had to be encouraged. Previous experience had shown that short-term and unorganized participation would not be sufficient in maintaining continuous pressure on the state institutions, and that the organized involvement of the people was the only guarantee that the company would fulfill its commitments if some agreement were reached. This led the Committee to attempt to involve several of the already existing grassroots organizations in the region in the electricity issue. To this end they drew on and promoted community events and other forums for discussion and made use of small community-based newspapers published in the area. Meetings and assemblies for the discussion and generation of new knowledge were also promoted.

The Methodology: Some Considerations

In contrast to conventional research exercises, which use different theoretical frameworks to generate knowledge that reflects as faithfully as possible the reality to be interpreted, the participatory action-research exercise undertaken by the Villarrica Users Committee (with the support of some outside collaborators) was aimed at generating knowledge that would also point to the proper course of action. Developing this knowledge would also per force involve personal and social changes. This, in and of itself, had to have profound implications for the method, as it assumed that the ways in which knowledge would be generated would have an immediate impact on the dynamics of community life.

In other words, it was not only a matter of generating knowledge on the electricity problem; both the process of generating knowledge and the knowledge itself would have a liberating effect. This meant using a methodology that met two criteria. First, at the rational level it must be capable of unleashing the people's pent-up knowledge, and in so doing liberate their hitherto stifled thoughts and voices, thus stimulating their creativity and developing their analytical and critical capacities. That is, a research experience had to be set in motion which would develop the participants' potential so that they would not only see reality for what it is but do so with a view to changing their place and role within it. If in suffering the reality, participants also discovered what made it tick, it would be possible to experience it differently.

Second, at the emotional level, the process had to be capable of releasing feelings, of tearing down the participants' internal walls in order to free up energy for action. A methodology was needed that would stir up both levels—the rational and the emotional—so that the people would link their rational conclusions to profound emotions.

But the process of generating knowledge also must have a mobilizing effect, reaffirming the people as actors capable of transforming reality. In this regard their emergence should result in the erosion of the power structure, at least locally. It was thus necessary for the people's word to take on an assertive power in order to improve their ability to negotiate. Further, the process of generating knowledge must contribute to broadening the exercise of grassroots democracy and to strengthening the people's organizations.

These conditions meant that priority would be placed on generating and collectively processing knowledge within two main social contexts, the first occurring in various types of community and regional events. The Users Committee promoted several activities aimed at involving people in discussing the problem and designing strategies for solving it. One night in late 1982, for example, the Committee organized a "march of lights" in Villarrica, in which the schoolchildren, women's groups and members of different grassroots organizations marched while carrying lit candles and torches to symbolize the right to electric illumination. This activity helped sensitize the entire town to the electricity issue through stimulating discussion within each family and in the community organizations on the importance of collectively participating in the electricity struggle. The Committee also promoted participation of the population in several cultural activities in Villarrica and throughout the region, in which different groups wrote and presented poems, plays and songs that reflected their perceptions of the electricity problem. One of these songs, "El son de la oscuridad" ("The Sound of Darkness"), sung to a rhythm people could dance to, was recorded on an album "Luchas cantadas" ("Singing Struggles") and became popular throughout the region. (It was produced by the Network of Grassroots Organizations of Southern Valle and Northern Cauca.) The cultural events proved to be excellent opportunities for the people to organize and disseminate their knowledge; this knowledge was creatively expressed through the population's particular forms and codes. But above all, since this process contributed to affirming their own culture, it moved people to become involved.

Meetings and assemblies, which periodically brought the community together, represented another context for generating knowledge. In addition to reporting on how the effort was unfolding, people used these activities as a time for reflection. Many told about their own experiences or discussed past struggles. This information was processed collectively at such gatherings, pulling together the pertinent aspects of past experiences resulted in a common narrative. The Villarrica Users Committee and the outside agents played an important role in organizing the information, promoting reflection, choosing and articulating key aspects to be integrated into a synthesis and selecting strategic codes to be used in designing the actions to be taken.

Collectively producing knowledge meant that many actors, coming from their own individuality, at different times and in different situations, and based on their own perceptions and ways of communicating them, contributed a variety of experiences to what became a common vision of the situation. These meetings, wherein everyone was given the floor, were a context for bringing forth their everyday experience, their significant images and common sense, all of which yielded a collective reading of reality, not from the confines of academic disciplines but from a holistic perspective. The possibility of forging new common ground—based on the people's analytical categories, their own interpretations, their cultural prism, their collective outlook and their traditions—made it possible for the people's subjugated wisdom to rise up while empowering them to transcend it to forge a liberating vision capable of stirring emotions and translating shared concerns into action.

The individual experiences, often expressed in the form of analogies, metaphors, sayings and anecdotes, were taken in by all the participants, who sized them up, contrasted and compared them and reaffirmed or criticized them. Accumulating observations, collectively selecting and synthesizing them while collectively drawing conclusions made it possible to flesh out the problem and understand it in its historical context.

Language ceased to serve simply as a vehicle for conveying isolated opinions—often the case when people respond in an isolated fashion in surveys or interviews—becoming instead the springboard for a new process of collective reasoning. The knowledge produced socially, and heard and legitimized collectively, was added to the people's ideological arsenal.

There were at least three "moments" in the research process related to the collective production of (1) a mirror-like narrative, (2) strategic codes and (3) the community's *pensamiento propio*— that is, their own ideological outlook. These "moments" do not correspond to rigidly defined stages, nor did the process involve moving from one to the next. The initiative did not stick to a timeline or a research plan; instead, it was largely conditioned by the pace of events. Receiving the monthly bill, for example, always led to much excitement and greater participation in the discussions. On such occasions reflection obviously centered on the content of the bills. On other occasions it focused on evaluating the actions. On the whole, however, discussion tended to progress through the above-mentioned levels.

Producing a Mirror-like Narrative

Such a narrative, which yielded codes for designing strategies for action, was a central aspect of the process. It involved the collective production of a shared discourse that reflected the majority of the people's individual electricity problems; it was thus a discourse with which the people could identify. There were two main aspects to this process:

(a) *Socialization of individual experiences in collective contexts (meetings, assemblies, forums and events), usually presented in the form of denunciations.* At these gatherings, the participants illustrated their particular situations through anecdotes; they often interspersed their opinions of the company and suggestions for action. Sometimes small groups used skits, poetry or song to communicate their perceptions of the problem. Organizing the perceptions and interpretations, and drawing initial conclusions, enabled the Committee to come up with an initial definition of the problem.

(b) *Expanding knowledge of the electricity issue.* The Villarrica Public Service Users Committee organized a campaign to collect bills, and promoted it through the region's grassroots organizations. This was done to ensure that the community would have a solid collective sense of its problem and solid evidence that could not be questioned either by company officials or the computer. They placed "bill receptacles" in several communities in mid-1985, in which people deposited a huge number of bills. (Once the negotiations with the company were over, the bills were burned in the Villarrica town square as a symbol of victory.) As a result, the Committee obtained a set of bills, in series, from some fifteen communities. In each community the Users Committees or grassroots organizations that were participating, advised by the outside agents and some supportive students from a nearby university, took charge of processing the information gathered, listing the names of all who had brought in their bills, and noting the figures for average consumption, the cost per kilowatt-hour and the cost of monthly use. There was therefore a sample for each community. While some samples were neither rigorous nor exhaustive, others amounted to a census which corroborated, with abundant factual data, the individual evaluations based on personal experience.

The information gathered was organized into simple graphs and analyzed in assemblies held in each community. Using different colored lines, the graphs showed the upward trends reflected in the bills, both in average consumption of electricity and in cost per kilowatt-hour, and thus in the average cost of monthly consumption per household. The graphs made it obvious that the company's "computer" was generating incoherent data, as reflected in the charges, and constituted solid proof of its ill intent. In some communities, for example, the people discovered that total electricity consumption had doubled—according to the computer—from one month to the next. It was noted in an assembly that obviously this was not possible; monthly increases in total consumption could not have been so abrupt unless everyone had simultaneously bought new appliances, which was not the case. In other communities the results showed irregularities in billing and very uneven consumption from month to month, suggesting that in many cases the meters were not read regularly, and that the company employees, either overworked or lacking access to all the homes, simply invented figures that were almost always greater than the true ones.

The knowledge generated in this process added to the people's original narrations, rounding them out with data and extending them so as to be representative of the problem in several communities. The initial discourse, fundamentally emotive and reflecting an ethical criticism, became a social criticism; yet it maintained its language and forcefulness. Part of the collectively processed information was translated into a list of demands, supported by the evidence gathered. This was the ammunition with which the people later entered into negotiations with the company representatives.

Strategic Codes

Detecting and reworking strategic codes for action was another important aspect of the research process. The collective narrative no doubt contributed a great deal to helping the people decide what to do, which was largely reflected in the text of the "list of demands." They requested, for example, that the company cancel the accumulated debts, adopt procedures whereby the meters would be read only when someone from the household was present and recognize the Public Service Users Committee as the representative of the community's interests in electricity-related matters. In terms of how to approach the negotiations, simultaneously mobilizing the population, there were valuable lessons on:

(a) *Collectively reviewing the history of the black population's struggles in the region and earlier organizational experiences, and analyzing previous successes and failures.* Drawing lessons for action implied not only a reflection on the electricity problem but an enrichment of their knowledge by drawing on the legacy of common memories of the struggles in which blacks had participated. Picking up on the long-standing liberation tradition meant reaffirming the capacity of the people and their ethnic group to defend their constitutional and civil rights.

(b) *Evaluation of how the tasks were being implemented through periodical assemblies and meetings.* This exercise, carried out on an ongoing basis, enabled people to learn more about the dynamics of their communities, the existing mechanisms for political control and the limitations and obstacles affecting popular participation on an extended scale. Reflection on the action made it possible to accumulate knowledge on the day-to-day processes, problems, fears and limitations involved in taking collective action. But more importantly, reflection revealed the key role of culture in its different manifestations as a factor of resistance to oppression and as a tool for strengthening forms of struggle. This kind of reflection made it possible for each experience to yield lessons on participation. On this level of analysis, priority was given to knowledge that, going beyond the facts and beyond the problem at hand, placed emphasis on the collective discovery of the best courses of action. This was the dimension that contributed most to the people's ability to learn more about themselves as a community, to characterize themselves collectively and to discover the possibilities that would be opened up by continuing their struggle through organized efforts.

Developing a *Pensamiento Propio*

A *pensamiento propio*, or own alternative ideology, was also a significant part of the process. This *pensamiento propio* represented a consolidation of the knowledge that was generated in the popular consciousness. It was important, first, because development of an ideology would make it possible to go beyond the immediate problem of electricity, placing it in the context of basic rights. It was also important because a *pensamiento propio*, an ideology generated at the grassroots, could provide a common grounding for different grievances, while at the same time serving as a cementing factor in bringing together different sectors and groups in the region interested in taking action to obtain redress for their grievances. Finally, developing a *pensamiento propio* was significant insofar as it required asserting concepts and values that the people themselves had helped forge in order to have the process become a building block in a broader social movement. Without popular participation in defining these concepts and values, they would not have taken root in their own consciousness.

In order for the alternative ideology to result from a collective effort throughout the research process, all forms of indoctrination and ideological imposition had to be ruled out. In this regard the *pensamiento* could not be constituted by a recipe or a set of formulas and slogans that the people could memorize and repeat acritically. Rather, it had to be a simple consciousness that would include the minimal and essential ingredients for further invigorating their struggle. Some aspects that were brought out in the course of events, and that became such ingredients, had to do with (1) defending popular interests, (2) the community understanding the true value of its own history and culture, (3) rejecting discrimination and oppression, (4) repudiating the traditional politicians and recognizing the need to rebuild democratic forms of representation, (5) recognizing solidarity as a value, (6) reaffirming the rights to the land and to liberty, and (7) defending the right to public services.

These aspects, which arose in the course of the research, were not discussed in and of themselves as clichés unconnected to the collective dynamic, but rather were reaffirmed as circumstance suggested them. These emerged not as a declaration of principles that could be reproduced and distributed, but as elements discovered and generated through participation which made it possible for them to be engraved in the consciousness of the people.

Some of the Results

The participatory action-research process described here yielded results at several levels. First, it made it possible to gather knowledge about an electricity problem, facilitating a successful negotiation process with the company. The arguments, collectively designed and appropriated, were incontestable. Defeating the computer was a triumph for the people, who demonstrated that "yes, it did make mistakes" when at the service of policies geared to resolving the company's problems at the expense of the poor users. It was only by making major advances in popular participation that pressure was successfully brought to bear on the company to bring it to the negotiating table. These pressures included dispatching letters with demands and requests from hundreds of people, periodically sending delegations to the main office, denouncing the situation in communiqués and articles published in small local newspapers and bringing the electricity problem before town councils. Yet, it was the collective decision to withhold payments of electric bills until the company agreed to negotiate, and to promote a regional civic strike, that tipped the scales in favor of the users.

Given the impossibility of negotiating individually with each of them, and wanting to avoid a worsening of the conflict that would lead to even greater losses, the company's directors decided to negotiate with the people's organizations.

The negotiations were held in Villarrica at a public meeting house with hundreds of users present. For the first time the people's spaces became the stage for negotiations. After several meetings—also attended by municipal authorities and some politicians, high-level company officials (including the manager) and community spokespeople—an agreement was signed which was beneficial to the people and which outlined procedures for the redress of their grievances.

A second result of the process was that it re-created civil society and broadened grassroots democracy. The process stimulated the rise and strengthening of popular organizations and the networking among them, providing methodologies for promoting popular participation. The Users Committees, for example, have supported the indigenous peoples' struggles for recovering their territory, and the protest marches of peasants from the Cordillera Occidental whose farms were flooded by construction of a dam. They have also promoted discussions among the peasants, encouraging them to refuse to sell their lands to the expanding sugar interests and to insist on access to the land. Likewise, they have stimulated reflection and action to confront educational problems and housing shortages. The Committees have further promoted cultural gatherings and traditional festivals that had been in decline with the stepped-up proletarianization of the peasantry. That is, the Committees have become catalytic elements of community life, promoting wideranging popular participation by encouraging community organizations and groups to go beyond their particular interests and join together to uphold rights that concern the community as a whole. The Users Committees have helped develop a regional network of grassroots organizations, which has become the basis for a social movement.

Extending popular participation has also led to an improved position for the common people in local power relations. The people have become aware of the impact of their organized action on situations affecting them, and have learned of the importance of going straight to the decision-making centers without the mediation of politicians and officials. This has been reflected in the pressures they have continued to exercise since the negotiation, demanding that state-owned companies be democratized by having community representatives sit on the boards of directors. In that sense popular participation or "people's power" has manifested itself in an attempt to gain control of and decision-making power over public institutions which, because of the progressive separation between the state and civil society, are managed without taking the poor into account and often to their detriment.

Finally, the process contributed to developing the people's ability to perform research and to reflect, criticize, deliberate, negotiate and cooperate; in sum, it reinforced their ability to participate. The real guarantee that the people will be able to continue participating constructively in re-creating civil society is their ability to engage in similar social processes, using participatory action-research. In so doing they reaffirm their autonomy and their determination to be protagonists in the overall transformation of society.

Conclusion

The Villarrica Public Service Users Committee's campaign for decent electric service was one of several participatory action-research initiatives that have been carried out by grassroots organizations with the support of committed intellectuals, not only in the southern Cauca river valley but throughout Colombia. Each experience has its own particularities and its own pace, depending on the specific conditions in which it unfolds and the techniques used. More importantly, what unites these processes is the effort made to draw on the liberating knowledge that flows from day-to-day experience, and is expressed in cultural and political awareness, and thus in an increased capacity to take action. Henceforth, participatory action-research can strengthen the social movements' ability to promote, from below, the radical changes needed for building a just and democratic society.

Chapter 5

YOUNG LABORERS IN BOGOTÁ: BREAKING AUTHORITARIAN RAMPARTS

María Cristina Salazar

This chapter is based on a PAR initiative, involving approximately 350 child laborers, from 1985 to 1987 under the auspices of the Ministry of Labour and the National University of Colombia in poor suburban areas of Bogotá. The project was undertaken with the collaboration of three officials from the Ministry, six social workers and the author.

One aim of our work was to establish the viability of more critical policies geared to the protection of child laborers (children and youngsters under eighteen years old), and to the gradual elimination of child labor. Another main concern lay in those organizational aspects that could further the promotion of a social movement organized by the young laborers themselves. It was expected that the aims and the paths to be followed would be discovered progressively in an open-ended process where better alternatives for action would be established.ed

The child laborers who participated in this initiative were chosen through visits to community centers of the Welfare Department of the City of Bogotá, located in households, family and/or cottage industries and in different construction enterprises where the children were employed.

Knowledge and the Research Process

The outsider participant team tried to be conscious of the different forms of knowledge that it was utilizing: How could reliable information regarding child laborers through their own participation in the process be obtained? How could access to their thinking and viewpoint about reality be gained? In the first place, efforts in this direction included the introduction of knowledge to child labor practices and legislation in Colombia and Bogotá among those groups of child laborers that were identified. Then all members together—outsiders and insiders—produced illustrated booklets, pictures and photographs dealing with child labor problems. Soundings on the children's knowledge about their labor conditions and related themes took the form of sociodramas, autobiographies, interviews and informal conversations. Reconstruction of the history of their families and suburban surroundings was also tried. The information thus collected was used for video tapes in which the child laborers contributed with music selections and other activities.

This effort to obtain knowledge about the children's own experience, opinions and beliefs was a slow process that required the establishment of more equalitarian or symmetrical relationships with and among the children and a development of trust with members of the research team. This was possible due to a persistent effort to communicate with the children to be present at their training, to chat with them, to listen to their stories, jokes and gossip and to share in their joys and fears. This meant a truly emphatic and *vivencia* attitude on the part of the visiting team.

For the majority of the youngsters, this was their first experience in which their own capacity for the generation of knowledge was stressed. Again through different pedagogical practices the team had to insist on their inherent capability to contribute, based on their own experiences, homes and urban settlements as well as Colombian society. The team became increasingly convinced that the ability of the youngsters to produce useful and/or pertinent knowledge was a real possibility. Much of our effort at the beginning of the work was geared to make the children understand this intellectual capacity on their own.

The child laborers then began to articulate their own personal history about their families and their origins. They related why they had come to the city, how they had become workers and in what conditions. They understood readily that the expression of their ideas and feelings, such as in the poems they wrote, was an element of the knowledge they acquired, and, as such, formed a justifiable basis for their world outlook.

Of course, the process was also intended to impart new knowledge to the children. The outsider team talked about human rights, local ethnic and cultural origins—in short, knowledge which could help to alleviate inferiority feelings and assert self-respect and self-esteem. This two-way formation of knowledge almost inevitably led to its systematization, and this likewise helped in the organizational process that was emerging.

The group then started to implement initiatives through images, video tapes and other audiovisual elements in order to communicate their new knowledge components. Their new self-esteem helped to strengthen credibility in regard to their own capacity for introducing change to their surroundings, and to stimulate hope for the establishment of organizations of young laborers which would promote a veritable social movement.

We therefore learned that knowledge was produced even under conditions of timid or weak participation and, moreover, that participatory actions can be furthered during the process itself when those concerned confront the results of their actions. When knowledge regarding child labor possibilities was transmitted to the communities and households involved, it increased the human mobilization potential. Thus one of the principal aims of our work was rather quickly gained.

Research and Culture

The continuous interchange of different forms of perceiving reality, values and beliefs, and of transmitting them from one generation to the next, constitutes what may be called "popular culture." This was the culture we faced in our initiative as we tried to understand structures of production and reproduction of popular knowledge, often invisible to us. We asked ourselves, how and with whom do the child laborers learn the know-how for their work, and how do they relate it to an explanation of social life mechanisms? Surely it is not academic science (Rodrigues Brandão 1983). Instead, we liked Eduardo Galeano's definition (1978): culture is "the creation of spaces for men [and women] to meet each other . . . all the symbols of collective identity and memory: testimonies of what we are, prophecies of the imagination, denouncements of what impedes us to be."

We therefore strived to engage the children in workshops together with the outsider team, stressing creativity, art, painting, drama, puppet shows and pantomime, in search of precisely those "meeting spaces." Through paintings, mud sculpture, stories and theater performances, we all contributed to this search so that the child laborers would understand the need to transform the dominant value systems, those which stress competitiveness, consumerism, sacralization of money, contempt for the poor and exploitation of the lower strata of society.

Discussions were also held with the young workers in which the team tried first to listen in order to encourage them to express themselves in their own words. Team members sought the children's own versions of their lives, their street conversations and friendships, their feelings and impressions regarding child labor and their relationships with employers and fellow adult workers.

Moreover, the team found that it was not alone in this quest. In one of the marginal urban areas in which we found child laborers (the Southeastern poor sector of Bogotá), we discovered several youth groups with similar aims to ours. Trying to promote authentic expressions of popular culture, these groups have been able to influence a large part of the sector's population. Through collaboration with these groups, and also with the support of art students from the National University, our workshops became successful in that a clearer consciousness of the young laborers' cultural identity emerged.

Finally, the youngsters were introduced to job training in such productive skills as breadmaking, carpentry and mechanics, not for individual advancement but as a collective or cooperative effort (as explained below). This activity became a rallying point for the success and permanence of the project (see

Ministerio de Trabajo-Universidad Nacional de Colombia 1986), since it demonstrated that PAR could be utilized with material and intellectual profit in productive enterprises. In 1988 the Ministry gave further support and continuity to this initiative by adopting it as official policy as well as increasing the existing fund substantially.

Intervention for Transformation

It was not easy to start and sustain participative processes with the children in the activities just mentioned. The participatory researchers, the child laborers and the families all are part of a long chain of transmission of authoritarian traits and other patterns of subject/object domination in our lives. Our socialization has occurred within strict up/down structural relations of domination which characterize Colombian society. Therefore, it was not as easy as expected to break with such authoritarian elements in the full participatory processes. For example, it may be easier to achieve a partial objective by proposing to carry out certain actions than by listening to different opinions regarding options and alternatives. Outsiders are used to "seeing" what should be done, and therefore are prone to propose solutions regardless of consultation with those directly concerned. Often the outside activists are under pressure "to produce results" and this may quickly lead to counterproductive effects. Authoritarian attitudes (even unconsciously) may thus lead to actions which reproduce current domination patterns. This tended to occur also in our experience with the children.

Evidently, the young workers were ready to accept current authoritative ways for establishing upper/lower social relations. They felt better when they were treated as recipients of knowledge rather than as knowledge producers, or as passive and subordinated units with little initiative rather than as intelligent youngsters, able to innovate and help solve their own problems. They preferred to be seen as persons who accepted indiscriminate orders, simply because these derived from positions of authority.

These attitudes in turn generated apathy and indifference in the young workers, manifest in their lack of organizational interest and absence from meetings, and in preferring to array themselves in such traditional set-ups as a formal classroom.

The members of the visiting team grasped the importance of breaking such educational routines so that a more participatory pattern would be forthcoming. This was the purpose of our intervention in the life of the youngsters and their groups. Positive results were quickly apparent, as described above.

A major conclusion of the initiative thus refers to the importance of such progressive changes centered on emphasizing democratic or egalitarian values against domination and authoritarianism, since they constitute the core of autonomous people's movements.

Skill Training and Organization

The initiative introduced rather novel ways of skill training as a means to achieve progressive changes. We wanted to support the labor of children, not under dangerous or hazardous conditions but in cottage industries to be managed by the child laborers themselves. Several of the adult members of the children's families collaborated in the implementation of two of these industries, a bakery and a carpentry shop. Some 150 laborers (mainly those above the age of fourteen) were able to participate in this work. They planned, discussed alternatives, undertook organizational decisions and eventually established four bakeries and carpentry shops under the new rules of self-determination and control. With the help of soft loans from a special Ministry of Labour fund, the shops have been functioning well after two years, generating income for the children and their families.

We wanted to support such economic and cultural organizations which would offer at least partial solutions to young laborers' problems. Within an organizational context it would appear feasible to implement participatory activities. Since some work in the community centers of the Welfare Department of the City of Bogotá had been undertaken with the same purpose, we encouraged links with youth groups in those centers to establish jointly the necessary conditions for the initial launching of a pertinent social movement.

In the PAR process to reach the goal of autonomy for youth groups able to create their own organizations and to influence their future requires continuous efforts by all those involved. We began to work patiently in the communities to which the child laborers belonged, mostly in the neighborhoods surrounding the community centers. Initial issues for launching a social movement with child laborers in mind were their heavy work schedules, the long distances they had to travel as well as the environmental conditions, especially in brickmaking and house construction. Likewise, exploitative and authoritarian attitudes among superiors and officials were targeted for criticism.

After their awareness was raised, the child laborers and their families were able to unmask the often hidden exploitation of their labor. It was then easy for them to transfer such discoveries to other authoritarian aspects of Colombian institutions and culture, even within their own homes. Of course, the changes achieved during the project were modest and quite limited in scope; we are aware that they are only part of the more fundamental ones that are necessary for social transformation at a macro level. But we think that some changes on the periphery will affect the social space of economics and politics.

Thus the base of a social movement of young workers in Bogotá was established through the knowledge and skills obtained, and through the organization and actions in which our young laborers participated. The unveiling of the latent political ethos of our work became apparent as the initiative advanced. As stated above, the movement did not come to full fruition because the visiting team had limited time. Now the organized children would have to carry on, together with their families and communities.

The aspirations set forth at the beginning of this essay nurtured individual hope and facilitated common effort. They stimulated a feeling of viability in collective and/or associated action. At least, the child laborers participating in the project now know that they are not alone, that their problems are shared by others and that they are capable of specific actions to transofrm their reality.

Some Notes on Participation

Again, it was not easy to obtain the participation of the child laborers in gaining knowledge over social processes. Several months passed after the launching of the idea, and only after they had put their trust in the PAR team and in their own capabilities, did the children begin to conceptualize about social and economic conditions. They asked themselves: What can we do with the knowledge we have acquired about social relations and labor conditions? How can we improve? How can we seek the support of fellow youth and laborers? These questions revealed new expectations which may be seen as results of the initiative's emphasis on participative aspects of knowledge production. Indeed, we were privileged to witness first-hand the generation of feelings of self-respect among the young laborers, and we found evidence of change in their old feelings of resignation. Passive and submissive attitudes started to give way to self-esteem and hope. But it was necessary to persist with them. These results underline the importance of continuity and broadening of scope in PAR efforts. There is a need to find ever new spaces for participation, emphasizing symmetrical relationships.

There were some other byproducts in this search. For example, the schools and cooperatives attended by the children started to reflect some of this horizontality. There were noticeable effects also in the self-management schemes for the cottage industries, in cultural activities and among the young laborers'informal groups in community centers. It is through organizational processes that the extension of participation can be achieved. New solidarity networks, a sense of community belongingness and new meanings regarding the public sphere are some of the components of those processes.

The positive impact of authentic participation for the development of the personality of the young laborers was another main finding of the project. The children were able to assimilate different experiences from those they knew, including the freedom and ability to express their own views about their situation. To be treated with trust and respect by the outside PAR team and other officials and adults, was an important condition for this achievement. Perhaps one can say that these child laborers were thus able to experiment democracy a bit more authentically.

The Colombian government, represented in this case by the Ministry of Labour, had not practiced with this type of democratic participation, in spite of the verbal emphasis placed on the general concept itself (Fals-Borda 1988). Participation was understood mainly in terms of social control and mass manipulation by the central government, so derived from traditional up/down development ideology. Of course, this developmental ideology has severe limitations. Thus it becomes important always to define with clarity what is meant by participation. In general, for us it is above all an egalitarian philosophy of life designed to break unjust or exploitative power relations and to achieve a more satisfactory kind of society.

Despite their official patronage, in our instance the governmental institutions involved in this PAR initiative did not question the radical participative approach which our team advocated. On the contrary, the officials involved accepted the critical premises of the idea, perhaps for lack of other feasible alternatives and in view of previous development failures. Together with us, they rejected some classical academic research techniques, such as sample surveys and questionnaires, which had proved of little use. We therefore found that there may be a margin for innovative action, even in state institutions depending on the technical and ideological orientation and personal flexibility and commitment of officials involved. However, the survival possibilities of these officials may be subject to changes of administration or to the whim of higher dignitaries who may see threats in such innovations.

Moreover, as youth organizations are more qualified and advanced in their material and intellectual objectives, they can become collective counterparts to official agencies and extend more authentic participatory processes. As Borja (1986) has said, proof of the participative will of a government derives from the economic and material support it lends to popular organizations, as well as from their juridical recognition, avoiding the imposition of dependency ties on those organizations.

The young laborers involved in this initiative demonstrated that a more authentic participation is possible when at least the following conditions are present: (1) a firmly based expectation of individual and communal progress; (2) the establishment of adequate institutional or organizational mechanisms; and (3) an active recognition by the state of human rights for self-improvement and collective advancement (Salazar 1987, 1988).

In our case the idea was not so much to attain such far-flung purposes as "revolution" to achieve feasible solutions to daily concrete problems. This does not deny the "revolutionary" potential of such changes, especially if they accumulate and acquire visibility in a macro dimension such as that provided by a regional, national or international sociopolitical movement.

Such a cause for significant transformation, of course, calls for additional organizational methods, resources and vision.

Under our concrete conditions, it is possible to generate a movement of young and child laborers through skill training and associative production forms. This movement may contribute to new positive patterns of social relations, leading to necessary transformations even at the authoritarian State level.

Chapter 6

ACTION AND PARTICIPATORY RESEARCH: A CASE OF PEASANT ORGANIZATION

Vera Gianotten and Ton de Wit

For peasant communities in the Peruvian Andes, the title of Ciro Alegría's novel *Broad and Alien Is the World* (1941) is still valid today. Alegría tellingly describes the heroic resistance of indigenous communities against the unjust expropriation of their lands and the permanent disregard for their culture. Despite the fact that Peru passed agrarian reform statutes in 1969 to break up large estates and abolish feudal forms of exploitation, peasant communities continue to be impoverished and exploited. Under these circumstances, the communities have developed different mechanisms for survival, resistance and struggle. Within this context, we began to work and to come to understand this Andean world that in the beginning was also "broad and alien" to us.

The present chapter[1] is based upon an experience of popular education and rural development in peasant communities in the department of Ayacucho in Peru,[2] beginning in 1977 and continuing to the present time. However, the political events which have occurred in Ayacucho since 1982, and which can be characterized as a "dirty war,"[3] forced the participants to change substantially some methods of their work. But the main objective of the project, which was to reinforce the communities' efforts to organize politically, was unaltered. The experiences we describe here occurred primarily in the first years of the project from 1977 to 1982.

Three basic principles are essential in developing a project of true popular education and of participatory action-research:

- Recognizing the potential for change in peasant communities as well as the positive and recoverable aspects of their economy, social life and culture. Our working methodology, therefore, was based on this potential rather than the negative and non-recoverable aspects, which are also all too evident in peasant communities.

- Developing educational activities with the full and active participation of the peasants. Instead of following pre-established objectives and goals, we worked with a sufficiently flexible methodology that would permit the peasants to participate in the elaboration, execution and evaluation of different activities.

- Creating a horizontal educational process from teaching to learning through a continuing dialogue between professionals and peasants. In that sense we accepted the existence of a critical consciousness on the part of the peasants. We started with the premise that both professionals and peasants possess a range of valid information. At the same time, both share critical and mistaken elements about the problem of development and alternative solutions. Only in an open process of critique and self-critique is it possible to develop these alternatives meaningfully.

We came to discover, however, that one essential element was lacking in our work. We were missing a major dimension to the relationship between theory and practice. Theoretically, we knew that the problem of "development" is a political one. Writings on peasant movements (Kapsoli 1977; Wolf 1969; Landsberger 1978) were sufficiently clear in this respect. But these works were analyses of researchers on historical phenomena and processes. They did not help us to translate theoretical assumptions about the revolutionary and political potential of the peasants into a methodology for educational work and promotion of economic, social and political change.

A critical dimension to our own experience helped us establish one more hypothesis. From the beginning, we recognized the importance of the peasant community and its organizational potential. We did not make any proposals to create organizations parallel to the existing community in order to carry out the project. This practice permitted us to see more clearly the political potential of communal and inter-communal organizations.

Our basic hypothesis expressed, therefore, the possibility of strengthening and developing communal and inter-communal organizations as political instrumentalities of the peasants capable of achieving the social changes they sought.

The present essay is not the result of a research project that has been elaborated in some research center. In other words, our work was not centered on the research or the researcher but rather on the action and the "beneficiary group." In that sense our work was not neutral.

Promoters of participatory research have abandoned explicitly the idea of scientific neutrality and argued that "the object of the research" has to be included as a subject. Proceeding in this way, factual data would be more reliable and greater objectivity in research would be achieved (Hall 1981). However, despite the fact that the principles of the participatory research have served as an important frame of reference for our own work, we have not used them as techniques to improve the quality of the research. Since our work was not designed as a research project, we were able to use participatory research as a methodological tool for action. We approached the problem of peasants' participation and organization in a qualitative perspective and on the basis of our direct involvement in the social and economic reality of the peasants.

Participation and Organization

Social researchers can select from the different major forms of such research—descriptive, applied or participatory—the one that promotes participation of the popular sectors. In doing so they will need to establish that their research in fact will lead toward the practice of social transformation.

There is no doubt that the new approaches of participatory research have overcome some of the weak points of the initial proposals of participant observation and action-research. Nevertheless, the fundamental problem resides in the interpretation of how to understand the necessity of organization. Participatory research has transcended the participant observation in relation to the researcher and the object as well as in the form of the production of new knowledge.

However, the structural effect that these approaches could have cannot be achieved in a restrictive participatory project. The limits of the project have to be transcended, that is to say, participatory research has to be placed in a broader context of political participation and organization of the popular sectors.

The political organization and the actions organized by the popular sector are, in the end, both a strategy and an objective of the participatory project—be this research or education.

Within the framework of participatory research we can distinguish different approaches or "participatory models," for example: the Thematic Research (Freire 1982); the Militant Observer (R. and M. Darcy de Oliveira 1982); the Systematic Devolution (Fals-Borda 1981); and the Participant Questionnaire (LeBoterf 1981). All of these approaches have been used in the project in Ayacucho in different phases of the process and with major or minor degrees of success.

However, carrying out participatory research with a commitment to the popular sectors is done not only through the application of a pre-established methodological model. A participatory project also has to be continuously sensitive to the kind of participation and organization being promoted in practice. In this way specific steps and phases can be changed and improved throughout the project.

The concept of participation is often focused on the insertion of the professional researcher (however committed) into the group under research and the participation of this group in the researcher's project.

The insertion of the researcher is an old technique of participant observation and does not guarantee that the research in effect is committed to the interests of the group under research. All too often the participation of the beneficiary group is restricted.

In these kinds of projects one often hears that popular groups do not display sufficient interest in participation. Therefore manipulative techniques are used in order to stir up their interest (for example, audiovisuals).

In our experience it is not necessary to come up with such techniques (often called "participatory techniques"), provided the popular group is responsible for the research.

In one of the communities where we were working, an acute problem affecting the already precarious economic situation of all the community members emerged. The problem was a disease fatal to all of their sheep, so contagious that only a collective treatment could be successful.

In order to attack the disease, the community members discovered that it was necessary to tabulate the number and owners of the different types of livestock. Therefore, the Community Assembly—the peasant organization—decided to carry out research that would document the economic, social and technological nature of the community.

The Community Assembly decided to establish various commissions in accordance with the issues to be investigated: a community census, natural resources, possession of land and livestock, customs and traditional (domestic) medicine. The commissions in charge of land and livestock possession were made up of community elders and young community members. The latter participated in these commissions because they knew how to read and write, whereas the presence of elders guaranteed an accurate inquiry since their status in the community would encourage all the families to give correct information.

Likewise, some of the elders were integrated in the commission customs because they knew about customs that were fast disappearing. In the commission for traditional (domestic) medicine, apart from the young who could read and write, handle a microscope and make some of the more complicated calculations, the assembly decided that women should participate as the key informants on domestic remedies and treatments used in the community for animal and human health.

When the information was collected, it was organized and analyzed. To give an example of how these commissions worked, here are the consecutive steps that were followed by the commission on traditional or domestic medicine:

(a) Systematic collection of information on the incidence of disease in livestock in the region.

(b) Compilation of existing knowledge about herbs and medicinal plants appropriate for the treatment of disease in livestock.

(c) Analysis of the causes of the disease. The professionals argued that the illness was caused by polluted water, whereas the community members stated that it was a punishment of the Wamani (the Mountain God). Both explanations were taken into account.

(d) Analysis of the domestic treatments. Analysis was done both in the field through empirical tests in the community (a field laboratory had been installed) as well as in official laboratories where the active elements of a plant or herb were defined.

After pinpointing which treatment served best to attack the disease and sharing the findings with all of the community members), an analysis was made to ascertain the most appropriate alternative within the framework of the peasant economy.

In all of this research work, both the community members and the promoters had a critical yet creative task, seeking out which advances in science and existing technologies could be useful in generating new knowledge through the acceptance or rejection of existing knowledge. The experience showed that it is not so much the simplicity of the techniques that defined the research as participatory research, but rather the fact that the topics, methods and implementation were all decided by the peasants themselves. They themselves systematized their experiences and generated new choices and new actions in a process of joint reflection. In this way they created, through a permanent process of education and research, their own intellectuals, educators and researchers. In the same way we saw how popular knowledge, empirical knowledge and myths and beliefs, stemming from the political and economic reality of the community, could be transformed into functional scientific knowledge.

The research was participatory not only in the sense that the population participated in it or that the research was based on popular knowledge and their social and economic reality. Rather, the research became an organic part of the community which appropriated the research activity as its own. We could clearly observe in the whole process that the role of the professionals was transformed into the role of facilitators as the community assumed responsibility for the research without denying the important role of the professionals.

Action and Organization

Another subject in the discussion on participatory research is action. While at the theoretical level there is agreement that such research has to be a permanent process of reflection and action, different interpretations emerge in actual practice.

- *An educational interpretation.* The action is referred to as an educational process implemented after the research has been carried out.

- *A developmental interpretation.* The research can evolve into a new style of "development aid" in which the existing problems are analyzed only at the local level, in the belief that the community can be isolated from the global economic context. The action is therefore referred to as the satisfaction of some basic needs without considering its structural dimensions.

- *A party interpretation.* The action is reduced to a political party action in which the researcher, as a political agitator, becomes a mere proselytizing agent, contenting himself with the number of persons he has been able to enroll in his party.

In the beginning we still perceived action as an educational process while research was concerned with applied research. When later on we related the training and research activities to concrete development projects, we thought it sufficient to organize the peasants around these projects. Subsequently we found out that action had to be considered as an organized political action. We did not, however, propose the party as the only valid alternative for organizing the peasants politically, but rather relied on the traditional communal organization.

In recovering the political and economic potential of this traditional social structure, it was possible to relate the research to an organized political action that went beyond the communal organization. In this way we were able to insert our program into an organized action of the peasants themselves: the inter-communal organization.

Often the mobilization achieved by a researcher, or through the projects that he or she began within the community, collapsed once the researcher left, especially if there was no established political organization to provide continuity. This can happen in programs that perceive the importance of organization only in relation to concrete project goals, or consider the party to be the only valid political organization.

The first approach separates participation in the program or in a concrete project from the peasants' participation in the larger society. For that reason, participation of the peasants usually turns out to be temporary, resulting in an organizational structure that has been imposed rather than taking into account the indigenous organization of the peasants.

The second approach also poses problems. On the one hand, there are those who work in a region where no such organizations exist and who believe they are doomed to work independently without having a frame of reference to a political organization. On the other hand, in those regions where there is political (party) activity, they will encounter a bureaucratic and dogmatic party structure that generally is not well disposed toward research activities with the popular sectors unless it involves indoctrination (see also, Arizpe 1978).

Participatory research and popular education are in a state of permanent tension, attempting to create an appropriate relationship between research and action. This tension not only presents a methodological problem but also an ideological one, and in practice it is difficult to classify programs of participatory research or of popular education in accordance with the type of action they are trying to promote.

A merely educational action can turn into an organized movement of the peasants. A restricted action of "development aid" can become a political action. A participatory project can be "reformist" at one moment and "radical" at another. Likewise, it can be "radical" in one political context, while it is considered "reformist" in another. In all of this, several factors, both internal and external, are likely to be significant.

In the majority of participatory research or popular education projects, models are applied to the participation of the beneficiary group, focusing only on actions planned by the institution promoting the project. This kind of approach is tied, explicitly or implicitly, to the notion of restricted participation of the beneficiary group in the society as a whole without aiming at a change in existing power structures.

Projects that perceive only restricted participation of the beneficiary group in the program can easily isolate the objectives of the project from its political context. They lose sight of the main question: participation in what and for what? In this way participatory projects can constitute a new form of "development aid" in which peasants are obliged to participate in something which is useful and important according to the conception of "development" of the institution sponsoring the project.

The objective of our work has been to contribute to the elaboration of a "participatory model" that helps to achieve popular participation expressed in political organization of the peasants. Therefore, our suggestions and proposals go beyond the limits of the specific projects to existing power structures in society as a whole.

Aiming at an organized political action means that participatory research interprets the concept of "participation" in a different way from more restricted projects. For this type of participatory action-research, participation is intimately linked to the political organization of the peasants in the larger society. In accordance with the objectives and purposes of popular education, the search for major participation by the beneficiary group in a project started by an external intellectual can only be justified when this technique leads to the emergence and consolidation of organized popular participation.

Peasant Organization

When discussing political participation by the peasant communities, it is necessary to explain the type of organization involved. In the same way that we argued the importance of taking the popular knowledge as a starting point for the generation of new knowledge, we urge that participatory research be based on and related to traditional or community organizational structures since these social structures have sufficient capacity to be transformed into political organizations of the peasantry.

In light of the actual conditions in Latin America, it is important to clarify why we do not limit ourselves to political parties or to syndicates or unions as the only types of organizations able to defend the interests of the popular sectors of society. The problematic and often conflicting relationship between popular education and political parties is due, on the one hand, to the reformist character of popular education and, on the other, to the proselytizing and revolutionary rhetoric of political parties.

Overestimating the role of the party, many political militants fail to take into account the fact that peasants possess a range of other organizational forms. Nor do these militants appreciate the role that these typically non-party organizations can play in the process of transforming power relations.

But popular educators, who would reject the bureaucratic and authoritarian domination of the party over their educational practices, often did not understand that they could not work in isolation from popular organizations. Limiting the organizing aspects of their work to organizations providing social benefits or assistance (such as mother clubs, saving clubs, credit cooperatives, communal enterprises), educators forgot that popular education can also include the politicizing of the popular sectors. Since it cannot organize the peasants around the educational and participatory objectives of a social change initiative, popular education is not an end in itself.

In order for popular education to have a meaningful political component, experience has shown that it must develop its educational work within existing peasant organizations. Effective projects should relate participatory research work to the natural or spontaneous organization of the community (as well as to syndicalist and party organizations when these are present in the area). It is not a question of creating new educational and organizational substructures. It is much better to try to reinforce existing popular organizations or movements.

The experience of a communal craft enterprise at Sarhua is a clear example of the importance of peasant organizational structure. We became involved in the enterprise through a consultation with a donor financing agency that had funded the enterprise since 1979. A community member with a great deal of initiative had negotiated the project with the agency through some professionals in Lima. The principal craft of Sarhua, painted panels of wood expressing communal celebrations and customs, was little known, and the few shops that sold the panels in the capital obtained them from some former community members who had migrated to Lima. Prices were rather high since the shops demanded high profit margins. The agency followed an operating principle that they only financed beneficiary groups directly and did not work with professional promoters in the community. But the agency did rely on professionals in Lima and on the as yet unsubstantiated premise that the promotion of communal enterprises would support productive activity and other organized aspects of community life.

Although there is a collective organization in the peasant community, this does not mean that economic activities can be collective. In reality economic activity is based on the domestic family unit. So there is a dialectical relationship between the individual family and the collectivity of the peasant community.

Furthermore, the peasant economy is characterized by a low level of specialization of tasks. At the level of the domestic unit, activities are organized according to the agricultural and cattle-breeding calendar. Within the community there might be some members with little access to other productive resources who give more time to some "specialized" activities. And the majority of the peasants in Sarhua do work at crafts (or selling labor in the city) in periods of reduced agricultural and cattle-breeding activity.

In craft production the whole peasant family fulfills various functions. But craft-related activity is not a constant continuous economic activity. Only during certain months of the year are crafts produced. Nor is it a sufficiently specialized activity that production of crafts in a collective form would offer scale advantages.

Sarhua was a very well-organized community with communal authorities and peasant leaders that were respected by all the community members. But the community member, who lived in Lima and undertook to negotiate the project, did so without the understanding or consent of the community. The project was initiated without any significant local involvement.

Outside of the communal organization, only some festivities that accompanied the project in the inauguration and some "evaluation" visits of the financing agency were remembered by the community.

Thus the project lost its first objective, that of being a communal project, since there was no communal control or management. Even if this could have been developed through a process of training and reflection, a fundamental problem remained—the concept of craft production as a collective activity. We therefore started to make an analysis of the problems in craft production—its potentialities and different aspects of the production process as a whole (from the purchase of raw material through to marketing)—with the community members through training courses and group discussions.

From the analysis some important conclusions were drawn:

- Craft production was only partially set aside for the market, the other part being for domestic use.

- Craft production was considered as a complementary activity within the peasants' family economy. All of the community members were producers of crafts, but nobody was exclusively dedicated to this activity.

- The principal problems of craft production were not so much centered around the production itself, but rather around the purchase of the raw material and the marketing. It was, for example, difficult to obtain wool to knit ponchos and woolen clothes, and every community member had to travel long distances to buy it. By overcoming this problem major surpluses could be produced, but in order to market them neither the community nor the enterprise funded by the donor agency had appropriate mechanisms.

- Activities undertaken through this project had little to do with the solution of these problems. In the enterprise workshops with textile mills for weaving had been installed, but investments were of little use since community members had their own looms in their homes. The functions also had been specialized. The promoter of the project was also the manager of the enterprise, and the craft activity itself was divided between laborers for weaving and laborers for panel painting. This division of labor could be worked out financially, as the agency paid the salaries. However, the labor division did not have anything to do with the needs of the craft activity, and indeed threatened the existence of proletarianized peasants.

- The eight peasants who worked in the "enterprise" left the agricultural and cattle-breeding activities to their families in order to obtain a good salary as a "craft laborer." Therefore, not only was the enterprise an expensive undertaking for the financing agency; it did not generate any jobs and even less capital. And because it was planned as a *communal* enterprise, it caused a whole series of conflicts inside the community.

After having analyzed the specific errors that were committed and the existing problems in craft production in general, the peasants and the professionals planned to reorganize the enterprise with two main tasks: the purchase of the raw materials and the marketing of products. The reorganized communal enterprise left the production itself in the hands of the peasant families that could produce crafts in accordance with their individual needs, but acquired raw materials and marketed the final products in a collective way. In the production process, assistance and training would be offered in order to increase the quality of the craft products.

This alternative was a result of evaluation and analysis by the peasants and the professionals of the main problems of the community. All recognized that the marketing was a central problem to the production of crafts. The community also sought more negotiating power with the larger society through the enterprise, which became an organic part of the community. Provided that we did not try to alter "from above" the basis of the peasant economy in either its organizational or its productive aspects, it was possible under this alternative to increase the economic potential of the peasant community. In the discussions and workshops, community members soon discovered that the reorganized communal enterprise could also perform well in cattle-breeding and other agricultural activities through both the collective marketing of products and the collective purchase of inputs.

During the whole process, the professionals did not do anything other than stimulate and assist in making a thorough analysis of the actual functioning of the enterprise and its future possibilities. More complicated or technical functions, such as financial accounting, were left to the professionals who later trained the leaders to handle these tasks themselves. The reorganization proposal did not contemplate specific activities for the professionals. Community members, accustomed to working within communal organizational structures, were perfectly capable of managing this form of collective production and marketing, provided that it was in accordance with established patterns of social organization of work under the control of the communal assembly.

This experience of the relationship of popular education, participatory research and a participatory development project with existing popular organizations—be they spontaneous, traditional or organic—helps to overcome the pessimism of popular educators as far as class consciousness and disposition to organize is concerned.

In many Third World countries, there are complex social relationships involved in productive activity. Neither the peasants nor the dominant sectors are clearly positioned as the fundamental forces of society. Therefore, it is necessary to begin with an understanding of existing social groups and organizational structures in the local community and the economic rationality which guides the lives of the people of the community. Equally important is recognizing the distinctive character and collective experience of each community and thereby resisting the temptation to impose ideas or approaches that may have worked elsewhere.

It is to these existing social groups and organizational structures that participating research must relate. Truly effective instrumentalities for change and resistance must emerge from the specific organizational experience of the peasants. In this way they will have the ability to resist actively and in an organized way those proposals for change that do not take into account their immediate and historic interests as a social group. At the same time, it is through such organized political action that peasant communities carry on the struggle for change in the existing power structures.

Concluding Notes: The Importance
of Permanent Reflection

In the concrete examples that we have described above, we have been able to observe how difficult it is to characterize a participatory program of popular education without taking into account the process through which the program passes. The relationship between the members of the outside institution or agency and the so-called "beneficiary group" changes in each of the different stages. By description and analysis of this process, it is possible to clarify various theoretical concepts and establish different practices of participatory research and other participatory programs of rural development.

As stated in an UNRISD study, the concept of "participation" cannot be identified as an "actual social reality" (UNRISD 1981: 5). Rahman also supports the proposition that, considering the complexity of participation, this concept can be explored but not explicated through a formal definition (Rahman, 1981: 43). We have seen through our own experience that there is no one model appropriate to all types of participatory programs. Nevertheless, we can make some generalizations about methodologies that have been used and about the underlying ideology in each methodology.

Van Heck observes (1979: 33) that a characteristic of participatory programs is that they are based on a methodology and not an ideology. However, this statement denies that the form of participation and the type of organization being promoted by these programs are shaped by ideology. In other words, an ideology underlies every methodology.

We pointed out, for example, that programs of popular education are often in tension with political action. This tension is not only a methodological problem but also an ideological and a political problem. In this chapter we have attempted to demonstrate that it is not at all easy to bring into line educational practice and research with the theoretical analyses or the political statements. Nevertheless, we have also tried to demonstrate that it is possible to connect restricted objectives of peasant participation and organization with a more global objective, which is the political organization of the peasants in the larger society. A third aspect that we have pointed out is that the achievement of this political objective is a long process of moving forward and back, because of a continuing tension between theory and concrete practice.

The analysis of our own experience has shown that the ultimate goal of our educational and research work can only be the formation and strengthening of peasant organization within emerging popular movements. Therefore, we searched for a means of transcending the relationship between the professional and the peasant so that we would arrive at a new level that would lead to the participation of the intellectual in the process of change.

Our theoretical concepts of participatory research and our educational practice met in a coherent theoretical-practical work project, where participation was understood as "the strengthening and the support of the standing communal order . . . [through which] the experiences [of the peasants], and their organizational practices aiming at the affirmation of their rights and struggles give rise . . . with the support . . . of the agents of popular education [to] the popular movements . . . "(Rodrigues Brandão 1983: 101). In order to participate effectively in the process, it has been necessary to analyze the different contributions made by "popular knowledge," "critical consciousness" and the "organic intellectual." This approach will only be successful if we start from the peasants' point of view and if we insert ourselves into the existing indigenous organization.

If we aim at peasant organization as the principal objective of our work, it is possible to avoid errors and limitations in popular education and participatory research.

That lesson emerges clearly from our described concrete experience in five years of educational work and participatory research with peasant communities in the Peruvian Andes. We end this chapter by summarizing other important conclusions from that experience.

A critical element in the methodology we followed has been a continuing effort at reflection based on analysis of action. We did not start off with a pre-established model; neither did we know in advance what phases we would go through or any sequences. We did, however, constantly reflect upon our own actions. We established the same mechanism for the group of promoters as well as the peasants involved in the program. In this process we continued to be "activists" in the sense that concrete work was also performed in the field—education, research and promotion. The promoters, the known "activists" of participatory programs, developed an "attitude of research and questioning," reflecting constantly on their own functioning. Likewise, the peasants were never forced to participate in the program; neither were they organized in order to execute some small project without having the opportunity to reflect on their own actions and on the program that was intervening in their lives. Having created a space that permitted the peasants "to raise their own voices," we avoided prejudging our program as being correct, and we also avoided generating among the peasants a passive attitude of resistance. Catalyzing a "questioning attitude" among the peasants has resulted in a complete change in the original proposal, and also guaranteed that the peasants could assume the program as their own.

The continuous reflection of all the people involved in the process has meant that the peasants did not end up depending on an outside institution. As Oakley and Marsden (1984) point out, while many participatory programs emancipate the peasants in their relationships with some institutions in power, at the same time they establish a new form of dependency on the promotional institute. As we have seen in the analysis of our own experience, it is important to visualize from the beginning a future relation of independence between the peasants and the program concerned. By the very fact that in theory we understood "participation" as our participation in the development process of the peasants, it was possible in practice to review our relation with them in order to be sure that they would not depend on us.

Within the inter-communal meetings, we did not exclude ourselves as an institution with which the peasants might have a clash of interests. A strong peasant organization would also be able to negotiate with us about the form and the type of our participation in their development process and political organization.

From the beginning we incorporated continuing evaluation in our work. But the most important consideration was not so much the methods of evaluation as the objects of our evaluation. Thus we evaluated thoroughly such activities as the execution of the projects, the performance of the planned training courses, concrete advances in different phases of research and fulfillment of the agreements between the communities. Even more important were the questions related to the incongruities that existed between our educational, research and promotional practices, and our theoretical discourse on participation, organization and rural development.

Participation means not only the involvement of the peasants in the activities of the project. It means also that the base organization or project activities must be related to the political organization of the peasants in the society as a whole. We evaluated both advances and reversals and obstacles and facilitative actions, taking into account:

(a) The role of the promoter.

(b) The role of the peasants, both of authorities within the community as well as the peasant group as a whole.

(c) The role of the communal organization and its political potential and inter-communal organizations.

(d) The role of the institution that sought to change its role from intervening institution to that of facilitator.

This process of continuous reflection has permitted us to diminish the incongruities between our theoretical statements and our concrete practice. When we analyzed the logic of peasant production, we saw that it did not confirm a presumed inefficiency in peasant agriculture. Peasant production incorporates economic, social and organizational elements. As a whole, it represents popular knowledge based on historical experience with agriculture and ecology and on those elements in the peasant economy that can in some measure be controlled by the community, such as work force, controllable natural resources and cultural identity.

This popular knowledge does not represent a static world view; it has adapted itself continuously to new conditions and new situations. Nor is it a "pure knowledge," free of values of the dominant culture, since one of the most important characteristics of the peasant economy is its relation to the society as a whole.

Our experience has underscored the validity of taking as a methodological point of departure the positive and recoverable elements of existing communal organizations. Practice itself has shown that communal organization is capable indeed of shaping the social organization of production. It would not have been correct to impose new organizational forms supposedly to respond better to the economic, social and technological requirements of the actual development process in which the peasant communities have to be "incorporated." Furthermore, relying on the existing traditional organization is from our experience the most efficient way to achieve (1) the acceptance of the program, and (2) the responsibility for it on behalf of the peasants. There was no imposition of new organizational structures, which meant that there was no necessity to develop outside strategies and techniques in order to arouse the interest of the peasants or change their attitudes and sociocultural norms.

We have been critical in this essay of certain methodological proposals of participatory research put forward to provide an answer to "development" problems of the peasantry. Our experience has demonstrated the effective capacity of peasants to organize themselves in terms of both production and political action. Since our role was not one of leadership, it was not up to us to define organizational models and different ways of linking these.

During this century, peasants all over the world have been involved in revolutionary struggles, despite contrary predictions of peasant apathy. Although there are also analyses that prove the political potential of the peasants, all too many studies have been carried out in an effort to understand their weaknesses rather than to appreciate their strength. These continue to emphasize that peasants are "resistant" to technological change, that they do not have a "political conscience" and that they belong to a social sector which is eminently conservative.

Is it not us, the professionals, who do not understand the rhythms and forces of change?

Is it not us, the professionals, who do not understand this "broad and alien world"?

NOTES

1. For a more detailed analysis of the concrete practice and theoretical and methodological concepts of participatory research, see Gianotten and de Wit (1985).

2. This work in popular education and rural development was undertaken by the National University of San Cristóbal de Huamanga as part of their project of social projection. Teachers, students and young professionals of the faculties of Agriculture, Education and the Social Sciences participated.

3. It is not the purpose of this chapter to analyze the phenomenon of "Sendero Luminoso" (Shining Path). The authors have published a detailed analysis of Sendero Luminoso (see Gianotten, de Wit and de Wit 1985).

Chapter 7

GLIMPSES OF THE "OTHER AFRICA"[*]

Muhammad Anisur Rahman

Africa was staggered by a recent drought. But even before and without the drought, African "development" did not show much dynamism. This was possibly one reason why the drought became such a killer—neither material nor institutional reserves were there to absorb such a shock.

The international development assistance system is eager to assist African societies so that a calamity of the nature of the last crisis does not recur. There are few examples, however, where massive international assistance has generated a development dynamism in a country where the society has not mobilized it-

---

[*] The author is grateful to Philippe Egger, who was closely working for the ILO's PORP program with the movements in Senegal, Burkina Faso and Rwanda that are reported in this chapter, for checking the summary descriptions on these movements. This essay is a revised and reduced version of a 24-page ILO WEP Working Paper of the same title (WEP 10/WEP.48) published in January 1989. (Copyright 1989, International Labour Organisation, Geneva.) Reprinted by permission.

self. There are many examples, on the contrary, of such assistance distorting the very orientation of a society's development thinking and effort. Wasted time and energy is expended awaiting outside resources rather than on mobilizing domestic resources, depending on the foreign consultant to reveal his or her wisdom rather than taking initiatives based on indigenous knowledge and skills, or toward misusing outside resources, the accountability of which is often tied to formal spending rather than creating worthwhile material and human assets.

The only hope of generating an authentic development dynamism in Africa is through stimulating domestic mobilization of social energy and resources. These may be sensitively supplemented by outside resources, so as not to destroy or disorient domestic initiative but to provide complementary skills and release critical bottlenecks.

How does such mobilization take place? It does not take place if the State assumes the primary responsibility for initiating and implementing development, for then two negative things happen. First, the people wait for the State agencies to "deliver development." As the State depends upon international assistance, the people also waste resources, time and energy in lobbying and awaiting such deliveries instead of mobilizing their own resources and taking initiatives of their own to move on. Second, the State itself fails to deliver. This in turn is due to two reasons. First, on a national scale, it never can have the resources to deliver since its resources are comprised only of (a) what it can get from the people (a politically dismal prospect if the people expect the State to give them more than they would pay for), and (b) international capital flows which are never a full substitute for domestic resources. Further, State bureaucracies are typically constrained to display the needed dynamism, innovativeness and flexibility in their functioning in order to become the "leading sector" in such development.

Domestic mobilization can only take place (in non-regimented societies) through people's self-mobilization. This involves the people—in convenient units of similarly situated persons/families, living together as a community—getting together, reflecting upon their problems, forming some kind of a collective structure (if this does not already exist), and taking initiatives as a group by pooling their brains, muscles and other resources to achieve some jointly conceived objectives. Thus they develop authentically, a process described more fully in the concluding section. Such structures may link at higher levels for coordinating, planning and implementing action on a wider scale. The pace of such development may come faster if some complementary outside resources, by way of brains, skills and physical resources, become available. But a forward-moving development process need not be contingent on the availability of outside assistance if a community would resolve to pool together whatever they have to accomplish even a small goal. This then becomes a psychological, proficiency-enhancing and material basis for the next step forward. This is the people's own praxis, the promotion of which is the fundamental objective of PAR.

The poverty and underdevelopment of Africa is widely known. Not so well known are some of the outstanding and inspiring initiatives of people's self-mobilization in Africa and, hence, the potential of the African people. In this chapter information collected by the ILO's Programme on Participatory Organisations of the Rural Poor (PORP) on such initiatives in West Africa and Rwanda, with which PORP is collaborating (as well as the experience of an ongoing project in Tanzania) are presented briefly to give some glimpses of this "Other Africa." Reference is also made to an initiative in Zimbabwe which is presented by Nyoni in Chapter 8. The author reflects upon these experiences in the concluding section.

The Committee for Development Action in the Villages of the Zone of Bamba-Thialene, Senegal [1,2]

The zone of Bamba-Thialene in the eastern part of Senegal was struck by successive years of drought beginning in the early 1970s. The villagers in this traditionally agricultural and pastoral area became worried as their livestock was increasingly decimated, agricultural productivity was drastically reduced and even the forests threatened with extinction. Many travelled, and those who went to the north brought back chilling stories of the fate of the villagers there who had been hit even harder by the drought.

The fear of suffering the same fate generated an awareness

that collective action was needed to confront the situation. This resulted in a movement for collective self-development in sixteen villages in the zone, which is today spreading to other areas of the country.

The process started in 1975 with a group who had returned to the region from a trip to the north. As they dared not at first publicly pose the questions in a society traditionally governed by the village elders, discussions were initiated in the homes of friends. Some of the questions posited as a guide for the people included:

- Where would they obtain those products not available in sufficient quantity from the forest, e.g., gamebirds, millet, cassava, wood, etc.?

- Why was the bush not sufficient for grazing the animals?

- What would happen if they experienced the same kind of difficulties as the north?

- Why did the zone lack collective infrastructure?

- Why did they not have productive work over all of the twelve months?

The team then appointed a delegation to different parts of the zone to conduct a census of the population, livestock, supply of seeds and other agricultural inputs from the government store, and of all the collective needs of the population. The census, undertaken in sixteen villages that were served by the store, gave the people much to reflect on.

By happy coincidence, early in 1976 the nucleus team met an educated professional, who possessed a wealth of ideas and experience on people's self-development and had recently resigned from his salaried job in search of more fulfilling work. Visiting the group and listening to the people discussing their problems, this "animator" eventually integrated with them to guide their struggle. Toward the end of that year the first "sub-committee" was formed in the Bamba village.

The word spread to other villages, where people also became interested in deepening the survey and the ongoing analysis. Many inter-village reflection sessions were held, with sub-committees formed in other villages. After the establishment of fifteen sub-committees, the "Committee for Development Action in the Villages of the Zone of Bamba Thialene" (henceforth, the Committee) was formed in 1977 as the apex body of these sub-committees.

There was an initial period of difficulty in consolidating the organization when collective discussions were not culminating in meaningful action. The people were frustrated and most sub-committees remained non-functional or disbanded. But after a sub-committee of Bamba village started collective poultry farm-ing in 1978 with the subscription of its members, other sub-com-mittees initiated similar self-help projects in agriculture or animal husbandry. In agriculture the traditional use of horses for ploughing was found inefficient and was replaced first by oxen and then by cows. This increased the return from the members' investment manifold, as the cows provided offspring, milk and hides. Loans were provided to members in the form of cattle (with repayments made in calves), thus building a revolving fund to support newer activities. Fattening as well as marketing programs were introduced for poultry, sheep and cattle.

After an initial period of fully self-financed activities, exter-nal financial assistance became available and the activities were expanded. Training programs in management and accounting, adult education, reforestation for environmental protection and community health programs were added. The Committee, however, is wary of becoming too dependent on outside fund-ing, and gives great importance to the financial contribution made to the running costs of the various programs out of such collective projects as communal fields.

In all of this work, collective reflection has remained a most important methodological element. Much discussion precedes the launching of any initiative. In these reflections special atten-tion is given to the cultural implications of an initiative, to en-sure that it would not introduce a cultural shock but would be in tune with local traditional and religious values. "Develop-ment" in this sense is not conceived as simply material change but is seen as an evolution of the totality of the people's life.

With the assistance from the ILO's PORP program, the Com-mittee in 1987 initiated a people's self-review of their ongoing ex-periences, with sessions held at the sub-committee level and between the Committee and the sub-committees. The following are some of the lessons highlighted in the review:

(a) One should not await State action. The financial means of the State are limited in relation to the needs of the different zones. It is therefore necessary that each group reflect on ways that they themselves can improve the conditions of their life, search for solutions and generally take charge.

(b) The people have to organize themselves. Organization cannot be imposed from outside with rigid rules. While it is easy for a leader to organize the people, such organization risks being dominated by the more able. It is better to let the people gradually seek out the path themselves in order to reduce this risk, according to their traditional modes, and thus develop a natural process of discussion and review. For obtaining and sustaining the solidarity of the group, the process is more important than the result.

(c) Effective participation of the members is essential. Time and space is necessary for discussion and possible amendment concerning modes of thinking. This requires that the people confront and collectively analyze each problem in order to deepen a fuller understanding.

(d) One should first of all count on one's own forces. The initiative of self-development should necessarily start with the mobilization of internal resources of the group, including their capacity to reflect, their subscriptions and savings and their latent capacity to work.

(e) The process of self-development has different phases, involving a slow evolution of the everyday life of the people concerned, accompanied by the acquisition and accumulation of knowledge and other resources with a view toward achieving liberation from all forms of dependence. This process gives to all the right to decision-making, and insures that action is taken immediately without waiting for outside help.

(f) It is vitally necessary to avoid looking for aid at the very beginning, which kills local initiatives and puts the people in a complacent mood. Aid is necessary, but it should not inhibit the evolution of the group.

(g) Information and training should form the basis of the activities conducted by the groups. Training will respond to the preoccupations of the people. It will not reject traditional knowledge, but will seek to strike a balance between what is positive in traditional knowledge and modern knowledge. In this process new privileges should not be created in the form of a repository of knowledge.

(h) Information rounds out the training, beginning with the base—from the base toward the top and vice-versa—and facilitating the taking of decisions. Then the groups will spread the information to other groups in the country and beyond, thus exchanging and comparing their experiences.

(i) The base groups should be made responsible for their activities by starting with appropriate training and laying the permanent structure of participation in decision-making. The nearer the decision-making to the base, the more involved are the people and the more responsible they become.

(j) After a few years' experience, there would be reasons for satisfaction but also for disappointment. For group members, most essential will be to have tried something together and encountered the obstacles which, far from dividing them, strengthened their confidence and solidarity. The actions undertaken permitted the launching of others, initially not considered feasible when the people doubted, or were even unaware of, their capabilities as agents of change.

The Six-S Movement in West Africa[3, 4, 5]

In Burkina Faso there has been a tradition of mutual cooperation and community work in what are known as "Naam" groups, which are specifically youth groups among the Mossi people. In 1976 a group of Naam leaders and some of their European friends formed the "Six-S" Association[*] to address the

---

[*] "Six-S" stands for the more elaborate French phrase: Se servir de la saison sèche en Savane et au Sahel ("Making good use of the dry season in the Savanna and the Sahel").

question: "How can one take as much advantage as possible of the time available during the dry season?" The dry season in the Sahel region is long—October to May—when the rate of un-employment of the labor force is high, explaining much of the poverty of the peasantry and the migration of their youth to the urban areas.

In addressing this basic economic question, Six-S held the view that "all action should start from what the peasants are, what they know, what they can do, where they live and what they want."

With motivational work and external resource assistance, Six-S has today developed into the largest people's self-develop-ment movement in Africa. Its headquarters are in Burkina Faso, where the movement began, and where it has (as of March 1987) more than 2,000 groups, with an average of fifty members each in thirty-three zones, of which about 800 are women's groups. Each Six-S zone is under the direction of one official coming from the ranks of the peasantry, who is paid by Six-S for the eight dry months of each year. The official is given one or more training courses in animation and technical skills, and is assisted by a management committee elected by the Naam groups in the zone. The apex body of Six-S, a council of administration, is composed of seven founder members and the zone officials.

Basically, Six-S is promoting the development of the tradi-tional Naam groups into progress-oriented organizations, stimulating them to maximize the mobilization of their internal resources and supplying technical, material and financial assis-tance to release critical bottlenecks. The local groups themselves define their programs of activities, which are concentrated in the dry, hitherto slack, season. These include:

- Group income-generating activities, such as vegetable gar-dening, stock farming, handicrafts, millet mills, grain banks, production and sale of horsecarts, fencing and so forth.

- Activities of communal benefit, such as constructing water dams and dikes, anti-erosion works, wells, afforestation—most of which contribute significantly in raising the produc-tion of cereals in the rainy season also.

- Social activities, such as rural pharmacies, primary health care, schools, theater and the like.

Six-S provides credit to partially support a large number of such activities. Activities of communal benefit are subsidized through limited cash remuneration and food in exchange for work, and a free supply of any needed equipment. In turn, Six-S gets funds from member groups' contributions and external donors. All Six-S groups have a savings fund built with member subscriptions and receipts from income-generating activities. As a matter of policy, Six-S's financial assistance to any group decreases over time with the growth of the groups' collective fund and assets.

A particularly innovative dimension of Six-S's work is in the area of skills promotion. When some members of Six-S's groups master a certain technique or technology, they form a mobile "labor-yard" school to teach the skill to other groups. Such mobile schools exist in each of the thirty-three zones of Six-S, and every group in a zone can request the schools to supply on-the-spot training. Through this process new skills are spreading fast among Six-S groups in all kinds of fields, for example, agriculture, handicrafts, health care and well construction and maintenance.

In addition, farmer-technicians are employed by Six-S during the slack season to advise the groups and assist in their activities. The groups can also propose to have one or more of their members trained in a certain field, Six-S arranges the desired training with some other group under apprenticeship or at some specialized institution. Overall, Six-S strongly encourages and facilitates the interaction between its groups for the exchange of experience and knowledge, and is also organizing exchanges between countries. Self-evaluation of experiences the Six-S groups is being promoted with the assistance of ILO's PORP program as a key educational and human developmental method.

The visible improvement in employment, income and socioeconomic security in the villages covered by Six-S (accompanied by a drastic reduction of youth migration from these villages), and the demonstration of such fulfilling self-mobilization by the people, is contributing to a fast growth of Six-S groups. The movement has spread into Senegal,[5] Mali and Mauritania as well, and is also linking with other self-mobilization-oriented peasant organizations in these countries. Today initiative has also been taken to introduce the Six-S regional movement in Niger and Chad.

From Twese Hamwe to ADRI, Rwanda[6, 7]

In 1979 an agronomist (hereafter, the promoter or facilitator) initiated "animation" work with the people of Murambi in the Giciye Commune of Kabaya district in Rwanda. His aim was to generate awareness among the people about their potentials and to stimulate action toward their self-development.

Informal groups and a tradition of mutual cooperation had already existed in the area. The promoter's work soon stimulated twenty-five peasant women, who had been informally organized since 1976, to constitute a cooperative called Twese Hamwe with some forty members.

Twese Hamwe first initiated collective activities in the agricultural field—collective production of vegetables, maize and the like—on land lent by the commune or rented. Gradually other activities were launched, such as marketing, milling, a rural pharmacy, artisanal production of baked bricks, a grocery store, grain storage facilities, poultry farming and other ventures.

Observing these initiatives, two other women's groups pooled their savings, and with the help of the promoter managed to obtain some external credit from an agency to set up another grinding mill that they managed themselves.

Other groups in Giciye and another commune, Gaseke, also interested in initiating such activities, approached the promoter for help. A general meeting was convened of all interested groups in the two communes—seventeen in all. After a few weeks, a second meeting was held and an inter-group organization, Impuzamiryango Tuzamuke Twese (ITT), was formed with two representatives from each group making up its council. The task of ITT, defined as a peasant organization for assisting its members, was threefold: (1) to study action proposals of the member groups; (2) to grant credits to the groups for launching their projects; and (3) to offer various other related services.

Twelve groups joined the ITT, a total membership of almost 300, with membership of individual groups ranging from six to seventy. This included three exclusively women's groups, totaling 159 members.

Numerous people's collective initiatives have sprung up in the two communes since then. Initial actions were generally undertaken in agriculture, comprised of collective production of cash crops to gain cash. Tree cultivation (cypress, eucalyptus, apple, tea) was very popular with nearly all of the groups engaged in one or more community afforestation projects each. Some other activities gradually initiated were grain storage, a consumer store, livestock, marketing, furniture-making, brick-making, one more mill (set up jointly by four groups) and the manufacture and sale of beer. The mill particularly was a great boon to the women, as the closest mill-grinding facility was a distance of twenty kilometers, with the result that the women were forced to spend considerable time and energy in manual grinding. Another met need was the opening of a rural pharmacy by several groups together, thus eliminating long walks to urban centers.

Yet another innovation was the establishment of a savings and credit system for the people. The savings of all groups were initially deposited in the Banque Populaire, which had been opened in Kabaya in 1978. But due to lack of legal status the groups had no access to bank credit facilities to finance their projects, and through the bureaucratic high-handedness of the bank officials, they encountered difficulty even in withdrawing their own deposits. Therefore, the groups sought an alternative solution. After analyzing the problems, it was decided to set up their own autonomous system of savings and credit, the Caisse de Solidarité (Solidarity Bank). Members' deposits are advanced as credit to the groups. Deposits earn a 3 percent rate of interest per annum, with credit extended at 10 percent.

The Solidarity Bank plays a particularly important role in the management of external funds for group projects. External funds to support income-earning activities for the groups are now channeled through the bank, and are considered to be the collective liability of all the groups and not only of the group using them. This serves the dual purpose of providing a credible guarantee to the donor against default, and also a wider collective interest that the activity of every group financed by external credit is managed properly in order to generate the income to enable repayment. Credit from the Solidarity Bank has so far been given for the purchase of mills, to set up revolving funds for one group and another for a pharmaceutical store, for the purchase of livestock for family breeding and for the improvement of housing.

On the basis of the experience in Kabaya district, the promoter and other colleagues and members of ITT established contact with other groups of the rural poor in the country interested in learning and adopting the methods followed. This led to the formation of an agency called Action pour le Développement Rural Intégré (ADRI). The task of this agency is conceived as stimulating and assisting self-development efforts of the rural population. Four directions of work have been identified: (1) to assist animation work in the formation of associations of the rural poor; (2) to consolidate such associations through advice, training and exchange visits; (3) to facilitate the emergence of a federation of associations; and (4) to provide direct support to base groups on funding and implementing collective projects of a social or economic nature.

The actions of ADRI have contributed significantly to an emphasis on the organization of the poor peasantry, and the collective initiatives by them in several areas, and to the development of linkages among them. Assisted by ADRI, representatives of ITT visited peasant groups in other regions and explained to them their method of organization and collective action. This stimulated the formation of inter-group associations in two other areas. Several groups of potato growers in Kanama formed an inter-group association by the name of Impuzabahinzi, and groups of sugarcane growers in the Nyabarongo valley formed an inter-group association, Abihuje. Abihuje subsequently asked ADRI to assist them in community animation work and in training and research on the processing and marketing of sugarcane.

ADRI also contributed to the creation in 1983 of an inter-group fund, Fondation Abbé Gervais Rutunganga (FAGR), covering groups of peasantry in Karago and Giciye which total more than 2,300 in number. The fund is built by donations from the peasants in cash or kind, particularly at harvest time, and is used to serve as a distress insurance to the members of FAGR against such events as death, fire, natural disasters, accident, sickness or an inability to finance secondary education of children.

Officially registered in 1985, ADRI is now actively working

in several other areas (Gafunzo, Muyira, Satinskyi-Nyakabanda, Lake Muhazi and Mboge, among others), assisting in the consolidation of local associations and providing animation work to develop awareness among the peasantry of their self-development potentials.

Animators at Work in Tanzania[8, 9]

In 1984 a government project was launched in Tanzania to "identify the planning and implementation needs of Tanzanian villages with a view of enabling them to initiate a self-sustaining development based on the villagers' own resources and ultimately fulfilling the objective of self-reliance." The methodology that was conceived was for a multidisciplinary team of researchers to work closely in dialogue with the villagers in thirty pilot villages in three districts. The project, however, degenerated into an academic research exercise, with social researchers paying occasional visits to villages, treating the villagers as objects of inquiry, all the while presenting papers in seminars and meetings for academic discussions without any clear purpose.

After drifting aimlessly for more than two years, the project requested the assistance of the ILO by way of methodological guidance to stimulate self-reliant people's action. The ILO responded by sending an expert (Mr. Tilakaratna) from the Participatory Institute for Development Alternatives (PIDA) in Sri Lanka, with which the ILO has been closely working to develop its conception and methodology for promoting participatory rural development. This gave the Tanzania project a radically new turn.

Fourteen "animators" were recruited in April 1986 from among the field staff of a number of ministries, having demonstrated the following qualities: a sense of commitment and a desire to live and work in the villages; innovativeness in work and a willingness to experiment with new approaches; communication skills, in particular the ability to dialogue, discuss and listen to the people; flexibility and a readiness to learn from one's own and others' experiences; and intellectual ability and emotional maturity. These animators were given six days of training in animation work to stimulate people's self-reliant collective action. The workshops consisted of no lectures but exer-

cises in collective reflection and analysis. In particular, this interaction analyzed the implications of two models (methods of action) for field work: one an anti-participatory model with
paternalistic development workers; the other a participatory
model with animators seeking to promote people's self-delibera-
tion and initiatives and thus learning from them. The trainees
thereafter drew up a program of action to immerse themselves
in specific village situations, to understand these situations in
depth, to identify basic issues of concern to the people's
livelihood and to analyze these issues with the people in order
to explore possibilities of collective action. They then moved into
fourteen different villages in the three districts to implement this
work program.

The difference between the "culture" of these animators and
that of government and political functionaries (who used to visit
them before) was immediately apparent to the villagers, who
responded positively by actively participating in the social inquiry and began forming groups and taking collective economic
action without any financial input from the project. The story of
what the Tanzanian peasantry can do when appropriately
"animated" is revealing and is best told in the following extracts
from a report by Tilakaratna:[8]

> The overall performance of the PRDVL (Planning
> Rural Development at the Village Level) project in its
> first year has proved to be very satisfactory in com-
> parison with the experiences of similar projects that I
> am familiar with in Asia. In most project villages the
> animation process has taken off and the methodology
> has been well accepted by the people. . . . The overall
> picture may be summarized as follows:
>
> 1. There are 63 active grassroots groups in the 14 vil-
>   lages which are in varying stages of evolution.
>   Some have initiated the first set of self-reliant ac-
>   tivities, using their own resources, and distributed
>   the benefits while channeling a part for accumula-
>   tion. Others have built up group funds and are
>   beginning to embark on development actions, and
>   still others have planned concrete actions and are
>   collecting funds to initiate them;
>
> 2. The size of these groups vary from three to 30 mem-
>   bers with a concentration in the range of six to 15.

About 30 percent of the membership of these groups is women;

3. The primary focus of group actions currently is improvement of production and incomes. Most groups have obtained land from the village governments to start group farms in extents varying from one acre to more than 30 acres. In the 1986-87 season, these groups cultivated more than 300 acres as group farms and in the 1987-88 season, the total extent of group farms is estimated to rise over 500 acres. Apart from agriculture, group activities cover a range of industrial and service activities, such as brick-making, timber and carpentry, blacksmithing, pottery, basket/mat weaving, grain milling, tailoring, consumer shops and kiosks;

4. All group activity is self-financed. Currently there is no dependence on outside finances except in the case of two groups which have obtained bank credit. Practically all groups have built up group funds through individual contributions (in cash or kind) and by channeling a portion of the income from group activity. The total capital accumulated by these groups as of the end of June 1987 can be roughly estimated at about 1.3 million shillings (that is an average of about 2,000 shillings [US$30] per member) and the planned accumulation of these groups amounts to nearly 3 million shillings (about 4,000 shillings [US$60] per member). These amounts include the group funds and the purchases of capital equipment for the use of the groups. Some examples of group activity and capital accumulation are given below:

    (a) A 24-member group in Ukwamani village built up a group fund by contributing one head of cattle by each member (cattle are a symbol of wealth and social status and are not used in cultivation). The proceeds from the sale of cattle financed half the cost of a tractor; the balance half being financed by a loan obtained from a bank on a guarantee provided by the village government. This group cultivated a collective farm of 69 acres using the tractor and assisted another group of 15 members to cultivate a 41-acre group farm. This second group is now planning to buy a tractor using the same strategy adopted by the first group. The activities of these two groups has created a demonstration effect leading to the emergence of several new groups in the village.

(b) A 13-member group in Mhenda village cultivated a group farm with rice. Out of the total harvest of 104 bags, 39 bags were put in a group fund, the sale proceeds of which the group intends to use for the hiring of a tractor and purchase of agro-inputs to improve cultivation in the next season. The pioneering effort of this group led to the emergence of three other groups which will initiate group farms in the next cultivation season.

(c) A 14-member group of women in Kimamba (a sisal plantation area), who had hitherto engaged in casual labor, negotiated with the local authorities and obtained a swampy land for rice cultivation. All cultivation work was done manually. Of the total harvest of 84 bags of rice, 14 bags were kept as a group fund and the balance was distributed among the members (average of five bags per member) which is adequate to provide food security for these households until the next harvest. This was the first time that these households were able to obtain access to such a stock of food. The sale proceeds from the group fund will be used by this group to hire a tractor in the next cultivation season, to expand the group cultivation and to reduce the workload of the (women) group members. The demonstration effect created by this group activity led to the emergence of two other groups (casual workers) who will also initiate group farms in the next season.

(d) In Kipenzelo village, 12 organized groups cultivated group farms totaling some 78 acres in the 1986-87 season. These groups faced similar problems such as obtaining fertilizer in time for the cultivation. In a joint effort to solve their problems, the groups formed a committee (called the Village Implementation Committee), consisting of a representative from each of the groups with an elected chairman. This committee negotiated with the village cooperative to obtain fertilizer on a loan for repayment after the harvest, and sorted out other common problems faced by the groups. It also identified the lack of a consumer shop in the village as a common problem and it was decided that each member-group will contribute three bags of maize to provide the initial capital to start a consumer shop. In addition, each group will have its own group fund to purchase farm inputs and to plough the group farms by using oxen in the next season. The demonstration effect created has led to the emergence of 11 new groups.

(e)   A 22-member group in Mwanawota village is collecting maize from the members to build up a group fund of 110,000 shillings to provide a down payment for the purchase of a grain-milling machine. The group hopes to raise the balance money from a bank with which it is negotiating, with the village government to provide a guarantee.

(f)   The context in which the above group initiatives are taking place has to be noted. In most villages communal farms and village projects initiated by village governments have not been successful and, in general, villagers have lost confidence in total village activity. In some villages coercive methods are being used (e.g., fines) to obtain labor for village farms. At the other extreme, the peasant cultivating an individual plot of land has continued to be of low productivity and cannot rise above bare subsistence. On the other hand, small groups which are voluntary and relatively homogeneous in character have proven viable in raising productivity as well as in accumulation. In general, the produc-

tivity in the group farms has been higher than
that in private plots as well as village communal farms.

To "guide" the above process after "training" the animators
in April 1986, Tilakaratna visited the project only once more, for
two weeks in September 1986. This suggests the basic power of
the conception and methodology of "training" of the animators
which was applied in this instance.[9]

Reflections: What Is "Development?"

People's collective self-development initiatives described in
the above cases (and the case of ORAP presented in Chapter 8)
not only point to a way out of the African impasse. They also suggest the need for reflection on the very notion of "development."
For a long time, even today, development has been identified in
many influential quarters with the mechanistic notion of the
development of physical assets and increasing the flow of
economic and social goods and services. Much of the activities
of the people's groups in the cases reported above are indeed also
addressed to such "development." But there is a fundamental
philosophical question—and the choice of the meaning of
development is a philosophical choice, a value judgement—as to
whether the process of the people mobilizing themselves, inquir-
ing, deciding and taking initiatives of their own to meet their
"felt-needs," is to be regarded only as a matter of the means of
"development" and not as an *end* in itself.

A value judgement concerning society derives its validity
from significant social consensus. Certain professional classes
and other elite quarters may have consensus among themselves
around the above mechanistic view of development and also
around the view that this is what the people—the "poor"—need
and want most. The people, however, have seldom been asked
to contribute to a social articulation of the meaning of development.

A study of ORAP (Organisation of Rural Associations for
Progress) in Zimbabwe by a team of four professionals presents
the following revealing observation:[10]

Significantly, the translation of the concept of development into Sindebele (local language of Matabeleland)

is "taking control over what you need to work with."
The names of most of the ORAP groups also reflect
these concerns. A few chosen at random are:
Siwasivuka (We fall and stand up), *Siyaphambili* (We go
forward), *Dingimpilo* (Search for life), *Sivamerzela*
(We're doing it ourselves), *Vusanani* (Support each
other to get up)....

In such simple phrases these popular articulations of
people's collective self-identity reflect deep conceptualizations
of popular aspirations and, hence, what must be viewed as
authentic development. The people want to *stand up, take control*
over what they need to work with, to *do things themselves* in their
own *search for life*, to *move forward while supporting each other.* The
different articulations link with each other as if they are parts of
the same whole. The present author with all his sophisticated
training could not give a better articulation of the whole which
is thereby expressed. One can perhaps try only to elaborate (in
the author's hopelessly elitist language): authentic development
is an organic process of self-propelled forward evolution. Some
dimensions of this evolution may be suggested as the development of a collective structure, to serve as an instrument of reflection and action; development of skills and faculties; a
progressively widening range of creative application of skills
and faculties in accomplishing self-defined tasks; and development of an understanding of this process of evolution in the context of its surrounding reality, thus developing as a human
personality. A community/society which would be moving in
this way, defining its tasks in favorable and unfavorable weather,
becoming engaged in doing them, and reviewing their experiences to promote their self-knowledge and asserting that this is
what they want to do—who would say that they should be
"developing" differently?

In such an evolution the concept of "basic needs" (food, cloth-
ing, shelter, medical care and education) with which much of so-
called "development" thinking and planning are engaged today,
become absorbed into a question of what the people would want
to create by taking charge of their own lives. These "basic needs"
are not to be delivered to them, but to be created by them, directly or through production and exchange. But the basic human
need, one may suggest, is not any of these. It is "to do things ourselves," i.e., to create, for being human is being creative, and this

is what distinguishes the human from the animal in oneself. The animal, indeed, needs to be fed and clothed and sheltered and medically cared for, and taught how to find all these, but the human needs to be fulfilled by creative acts.

The tragedy of underdevelopment is not that the ordinary people have remained poor and are becoming poor, but that they have been inhibited from authentic development as humans. In many countries elites in the first instance have appropriated the people's resources, and then have taken over the right to "develop" society. In others, indigenous resources may be at the command of the people, but the "development expertise" is assumed to rest with official bureaucracies and the technocracy. This has distorted the natural and profound popular notion of (authentic) development. For no one can develop others; one can only stretch or diminish others by trying to "develop" them. True to this maxim, the elites who are in charge of social direction have only "developed" themselves at the cost of society. This has been a brilliant performance—the evolution of elite capabilities, including the capability and accomplishment of mass impoverishment and underdevelopment the world over through domination, exploitation and environmental destruction.

One might even say that the very notion of "poverty," conventionally conceived in consumeristic terms, distracts from the human need to be fulfilled by creative acts. The first man or woman, or the first human community, was not "poor" for not having any clothes to put on or shelter to house the body. It was the beginning of life, to move forward from there by creating and constructing with one's own priorities and with self-determination. People become poor when their resources are appropriated by others, thereby denying them not only the basic material means of survival but more fundamentally, through dependence on others for survival, their self-determination. The communities, whose efforts at authentic development are reported in this chapter, may be "poor" by the material standards of the so-called "rich," but are immensely rich themselves in the culture and values they are showing in the way they are moving forward as part of a self-determined collective endeavour.

Some Further Observations

Philosophy apart, the initiatives reported in this essay are a few examples in Africa of attempts to reverse the process of underdevelopment. They are rich in lessons. One is that where some traditional culture and form of mutual cooperation still exist, the process of authentic development can start from there, giving those cultures a sense of aspiration, possibilities and assertion. Once this sense is infused, people's imaginativeness can provide the means to promote the satisfaction of the "basic needs," very few of which are conceived in conventional, externally designed and controlled projects. These include a collective fund as an instrument of banking and social insurance; a people's bank; collective marketing and storage; the pooling of human energy and talents—a collective fund of human resources— otherwise available for individual pursuits only in mutual cooperation and joint action to promote everyone's needs satisfaction; the spreading of skills from peoples to peoples; and so on.

An important message lies in most such initiatives being nongovernmental ventures. The essence of this message is also confirmed in the Tanzanian case where the initiative came in a government project, and the contradiction which emerged between the conception of the project and forces against it. It took more than two years of aimless drifting to realize that a drastic reorientation was needed. Mention may be made here of the experience in both Sri Lanka and the Philippines, where such field animation methodology was initially tried in government projects with equally inspiring results, but also where the field animators and facilitators saw the limits of working in the framework of government bureaucracy and formed independent organizations—PIDA in Sri Lanka and PROCESS in the Philippines (see Tilakaratna 1985 and Rahman 1983)—to carry the work forward. Limits in the Tanzanian work may also be soon reached, and the question of further forward movement of the initiative rests upon the possibility of forming an SPO with greater flexibility of operation to take over the task of animating and facilitating people's self-reliant action.

Leaving apart the work in Tanzania, which is but a small and relatively recent experiment in grassroots animation in which institutional unfolding has yet to mature, a noteworthy feature of the other cases of people's self-development initiatives is, indeed, the extent of people's self-direction and control of their collective activities. The Six-S originated out of the vision of the people's own leaders in dialogue with some outside friends, and is a people's organization with a few of these friends in the Council of Administration as "organic intellectuals." The Committee for Development Action in Senegal is a people's organization. ORAP in Zimbabwe (see Chapter 8) evolved from a conception of a few middle-class activists who, however, allowed people's structures to develop assertively and eventually to absorb the activists as "organic intellectuals," working for the apex body, ORAP, the majority of whom are people's representatives. The fact of such structurally organic relations between these two trends—middle-class activists and people's leaders—stands in sharp contrast to the relations observed in most South and Southeast Asian cases of such activism known to the author, where middle-class activists serve under a separate structure of their own, commonly known as NGOs (non-governmental organizations). This dichotomy between people's structures and structures of middle-class activists, who work to promote people's structures, carries with it its own questions of balance of power in the overall movement, of relative privileges, structural dependence of one upon another and the like. It is noteworthy that in the Rwandan case there initially also was no formal structure of middle-class activists for a considerable period, and work was concentrated on promoting people's structures and linking them with one another. While ADRI has been formed more recently as a separate middle-class structure to service the people's movement, it seems to have been born out of a felt need of an evolving and vibrant grassroots movement for some special services and was not, as in many other cases, a structure existing prior to the grassroots movement. This should, at least, give the grassroots movement a lead in the dialectics between the two trends.

The question of the relation between the two trends in initiatives to promote people's authentic development, assisted significantly by middle-class activists or facilitators, is important because the middle class can at best only commit one part of its being to the cause of the people. The other part remains committed to "middle-class culture values and aspirations." In this sense one is at most both a friend and an enemy of the people. The best possibility of keeping the negative trends in check lies in the control of an aware and vigilant people over every action. It is curious that in some of the pioneering African cases of initiating people's self-development, the "balance of power" seems to be more on the side of the people than the average cases. One would like to understand the social, historical and cultural factors that bring about such transformation, a subject perhaps for a socioanthropological inquiry and an agenda for the ongoing PAR.

In any case, Africa is indeed showing evidence of vibrant and assertive people's self-development efforts in rural areas, which are at the frontier of such efforts anywhere and from which inspiration can be gleaned and much learned. The task of promoting authentic people's development is perhaps made easier in communities where rural class polarization is not acute and land not such a constraint, as is the case in most of the examples presented in this chapter. With the sharp rural class polarization in most South/Southeast Asian and Latin American countries, initiatives toward collective self-development of the ordinary rural people are handicapped by generally stiff, often violent, resistance from elites (feudal, semi-feudal or capitalist), whose privileged lives thrive on the class exploitation of the under-privileged, coupled by the ordinary people's lack of access to some basic means of production to survive independently. In such situations collective initiatives by the people are often of necessity channeled into militant action to assert human rights and gain access to some basic economic resources (Rahman 1986, 1987). In the above African scenario, the main source of resistance to such initiatives would perhaps be the State and professional bureaucracy, the privileged status of which depends in part on the power they have either to deliver, or to sermonize on how to deliver "development."

We shall not comment on the State bureaucracy in this essay. The initial fate of the Tanzanian project, which was so tragic for the project objectives while being so lucrative for the interdisciplinary researchers, is symbolic of the general inability of the mainstream of professional intelligentsia to indicate any direction and methodology to promote authentic people's development, not to mention their unconcern over serving this cause. Genuine people-oriented activists coming from the professional class are as a rule exceptions—a handful in number in some countries, more in others. Yet persons of powerful societal vision, conception, intellectual ability and methodological skill for translating conception into practice are needed to provide some guidance and perspective to such initiatives, and for such initiatives to spread widely over space with some coherence. As the Tanzanian work also dramatically shows, and indeed as all the other cases presented above confirm, the people seem to be ready to respond to appropriate "animation," even with no outside financial help. Must this be left to spontaneous historical emergence, or can some method of "schooling" be devised to promote a greater concern among a nation's potential intellectual leaders to work *with* and not *upon* the people, so that the "Other Africa" could develop faster?

NOTES

Committee for Development Action, Senegal:

1. Marius Dia. *L'Experience en matiere d'auto-développement du Comité d'Action pour le Développement des Villages de la Zone Bamba-Thialene.* Report on People's Self-review. Geneva: ILO, 1987, mimeographed.
2. *Sharing Experiences in Development.* Report of a Workshop for Development Leaders, Silveira House, and Innovations et Réseaux pour le Développement, Harare, June 18-23, 1984, pp. 28-35.

Six-S:

3. A.R. Sawadogo and B.L. Ouedraogo. *Auto-évaluation de six groupements Naam dans la province du Yatenga.* Draft report. Geneva: ILO, August 1987.
4. Philippe Egger. *L'Association Six "S"—Se servir de la saison sèche en Savane et au Sahel—et les groupement Naam: note sur quelques observations.* Geneva: ILO, February 1987, mimeographed.
5. H. Teuben et al. *Rapport final sur les résultats de l'auto-évaluation assistée des unions des groupements des zones 6S au Sénégal.* 1983, mimeographed.

ADRI:

6. Siméon Musengimana, *La dynamique des organisations*

paysannes au Rwanda: le cas de l'intergroupement Tuzamuke de Kabaya. (Report on a People's Self-review Project.) Geneva: ILO, February 1987, mimeographed.

7.   Philippe Egger. *La leçon de Jomba, trois tableaux pour une conclusion sur l'emploi rural au Rwanda.* Geneva: ILO, March 1987, mimeographed.

Tanzania:

8.   S. Tilakaratna. *The Animator in Participatory Rural Development (Concept and Practice).* Geneva: ILO, 1987. (Especially Chapter 4, Annex: "Animator Training [first phase] in Tanzania.")

9.   Project documents in ILO files.

ORAP:

10.   D.M. Chavunduka et al. *Khuluma Usenza, the Story of ORAP in Zimbabwe's Rural Development: An Interpretative Study.* Bulawayo: Organisation of Rural Associations for Progress (ORAP), July 1985.

Chapter 8

PEOPLE'S POWER
IN ZIMBABWE

Sithembiso Nyoni

The independence of Zimbabwe came after a protracted war of liberation. During this struggle, the people were formed into committees through which liberation strategies were formulated. One of the main strategies of the freedom fighters was to create a consciousness within the people. This was done through dialogue and participation. Evenings were used for political meetings in which the people shared their experiences of oppression, exploitation and domination by the colonial regime. They also planned various strategies for resistance, gathering intelligence and other aspects of the total struggle. Women, men and youth all had their specific roles.

People's participation and conscious reflection on their situation became the motivating force for fighting on. Among other things, most rural Zimbabweans fought for their rights to the means of production, such as land and thus food and other economic necessities. They fought for freedom of speech and freedom to educate themselves. They fought to regain their dignity and for their right to be part of a whole nation in which they would take their place as full citizens.

In order for the rural people to obtain these rights, there was need for a shift in the decision-making process as well as in the political and economic power base. For most people, therefore, the attainment of independence was but one step toward the attainment of people's power. It was not an end in itself, but rather a beginning of several struggles for the rural people's total integration into society in which all citizens have equal rights.

After independence, it was recognized that there still existed some constraints which prevented the people from full participation in the process of their self-development. One of these constraints was the international colonial tradition that emphasized law and order in which the people were conditioned to accept their plight without question. Another was a deep tribalism which was created by the partition of Africa and colonial rule and which had been appropriated and misused by partisan politics. Such a divisive situation was not conducive to advancement and progress.

There was also a good deal of cultural, material and psychological dependence. This led to a lack of a sense of responsibility for using resources for the benefit of all. This in turn led to the absence of institutional mechanisms that could redress the imbalance between the urban and the rural, the rich and the poor. Oppression had thus diverted and polluted the best energies of our poor rural population as well as of the urban elites, including those who were part of the oppressive system, to the extent that they could do very little for themselves.

The development of a people with such a history cannot be achieved by any "system." Nor can a people's development continue to be designed and seen solely through the eyes of experts, who in the past have only been able to identify the smoke from the burning land of our people, but not the causes of the fire or how it could be extinguished. Thus in order to redress the conditions just mentioned, we needed to adopt new ways of work in which people's participation would be the key.

This essay presents but one example of several initiatives which were taken by Zimbabweans after independence in an attempt to further the people's continuous struggle toward regaining their power as well as to participate in the shaping of their future at the individual community and national levels.

The author is aware that empowerment and participation have become fashionable words in current development literature, the meanings and practice of which are often ambiguous and vague. There are many reasons for this, one being that such words have been appropriated by politicians and professionals for their own ends.

A Matter of Definition and Understanding of the Concepts in Practice

Most politicians and development practitioners prefer to speak in the name of the people. They also prefer to present "people's" projects as empowering and participatory in order to raise funds. In most cases these words have been used as a mask for "development programs." The casual use of these terms has, therefore, prevented people from questioning such programs, which has in turn prevented them from getting to know what is actually happening in any given development activity.

The people referred to are usually the majority of the population, often known as the "grassroots." Ordinary people, belonging to the poor sector that largely resides in the countryside, they are far removed from, yet directly affected, by political decisions. These are the people who should speak for themselves directly and not through politicians or development practitioners. Their rights and dignity cannot be restored through other people, but only through their own direct involvement and participation. People's power, therefore, refers to the energies of such people being released and channeled toward positive thinking and action in order to better their lot. Programs that empower the people refer to a process in which the people take control of their reflections and actions to shape their future.

Participation has been viewed either as equivalent to grassroots democracy or as a derivative of Western social philosophy. This type of participation has underestimated the drama that takes place when the people engage in a participatory process. It has not allowed for the consideration of contradictions and conflicts in any given situation. For us, the birth pains of participation involve surfacing, understanding and mastering these conflicts and contradictions that have led us to new visions, new relationships and strategies of work.

Participation has also been subverted into aspirations for solidarity more useful to the interests of the past colonial elites and their Western allies than for the poor majority. Such "manipulative" participation ignores the internal contradictions and conflicts which are part and parcel of a true participatory process. The author is therefore very aware that this kind of participation may become a mere conservative force, even a cynical cover for continuing the privileges of existing elites.

As defined within the Organisation of Rural Associations for Progress (ORAP), participation is a continuous reaction of powerless people to their national forces as well as major world political and economic forces. It is an active and dynamic process that does not try to hide what is actually happening. Through it, people become aware of the internal and external conflicts and contradictions as well as certain fundamental ambiguities and the dangers of those ambiguities.

Therefore participation is not a smooth, easy or painless "development" process. It is an active engagement in the search for one's own history and the part played by the individual and others around him in shaping that history. Participation does not apportion blame to outside forces as the sole cause of a people's plight. It helps the people examine themselves, their roles and positions in society, as well as the external factors in the processes of development/underdevelopment, those forces that are either facilitating or impeding their advancement as they see best. In doing so, people are confronted not only with the impact of the outside world upon their lives but also with increased awareness of the oppression, exploitation and domination they have been experiencing.

People are not always passive victims. Sometimes they actively contribute, creating easy conditions for domination and oppression to take place. For us, therefore, participation has become a process in which we question our total existence and those elements that make up that existence. What should this existence be? In trying to answer such questions the people attempt to identify very clearly not only what the outside has done to them but also their own contributing weaknesses and how they can overcome them. They likewise seek to identify their own energies, capabilities and strengths and how they can best harness and use them for progress. In a word, participatory advancement is for us a deep self-searching process which leads to the authentic development of a people's self-reliance and people's power.

The Case of ORAP in Zimbabwe

ORAP is a village movement founded by Zimbabweans soon after independence, operating in the provinces of Matabeleland North/South and Midlands. The movement was born out of two participatory research exercises led by a Zimbabwean woman. The first focused on future plans in response to the needs of the war-torn rural population.

The second was a study of the village committees, mentioned above, which were formed during the war. What role did they play in the liberation struggle and how did they see their future in independent Zimbabwe? Most of the village committees, which were part of this participatory action-research, formed the first groups in ORAP. Within a period of seven years, ORAP has grown from eight initial groups to 600. ORAP now incorporates over 60,000 families and continues to grow daily. Rural families and their members form the bases of ORAP power, and from here all aspirations and programs emanate.

The founding and the growth of ORAP showed that participatory action-research can be an active process in which the participants' conscious reflection becomes the active force for creative action.

The power of the oppressor is sustained through the exercise of economic, political and military power on the weak. In like manner, the power of the poor and the oppressed has to be created and maintained through resistance, awareness building, self-reliance and access to appropriate resources.

Zimbabwe has shown that participation and awareness building cannot on their own change the positions of power in favor of the weak. Other conditions and resources are needed to enable the poor to regain their power. One major resource is the creation, through people of like mind and from all classes, of solidarity links conducive to promoting people's power. Thus what is needed from all those engaged in such work is an authentic commitment to the people and an unconditional acceptance of the people's opinions in order to facilitate a true dialogue.

During the liberation struggle, Zimbabweans from all classes joined hands to weaken and conquer the forces of domination, exploitation and oppression through an armed struggle and other non-violent means of resistance and non-cooperation. After independence, the positions of leadership were taken over largely by the educated, presenting the strong possibility that the rural poor would continue to be marginalized. To avoid this, various people's organizations, cooperatives and movements sprang up in the countryside to mobilize the people and to create and facilitate the distribution of resources, especially those of land and capital. ORAP was one such movement.

ORAP realized, however, that the distribution and the development of physical and material resources without the distribution of power would simply lead to dependence on those who control these resources. Therefore the poor would remain powerless and superfluous to the progress of their nation. For this reason, ORAP places great importance on dynamic education in which people's awareness of themselves and their world is created.

Discussions and dialogue are key to ORAP's work and involve in-depth analyses in which, among other things, the people identify various connections that facilitate or hinder people's power. The end result of such an exercise should be corrective action undertaken by the people, together with recognition that this action must be continuously evaluated against actual experience. True participation calls for continuous rethinking and re-articulation of the whole process until the final goal is reached. This means that one program may be repeated many times in different ways in order to find the right solution to a specific problem.

Participation is not an easy process; it is complicated and often painful. Since it is also difficult to share or to explain processes, people are expected to seek answers within themselves. Thus the development process is delayed while change takes place from within. A few examples of the PAR process are given below.

When ORAP first started, groups met to discuss local problems and to seek solutions. Action would then be taken in the form of projects. All articulations, needs, problems and their root causes, constraints, solutions and needed resources would be grouped into two categories.

First, there would be those that emanated from within ourselves and over which we have some control, and second, those elements from the outside beyond our control. After such an exercise, programs would then be formulated and implemented. At the beginning, the rural people fell into the trap of coming up with traditional projects as solutions to their problems, for example, sewing, knitting, bread-making, poultry-keeping, carpentry and the like. These projects were largely meant to solve people's economic problems and small grants of $500 would then be given to each qualified group.

In almost every case, however, no economic problems were solved. Returns from such projects would be negligible as fifteen to thirty groups of families expected an equal share from a project in which only $500 had been invested. Apart from the meager profits made, more machines, tools or other raw materials were often unavailable when needed due to a lack of foreign currency to import such equipment, and because the rural poor were not a national priority.

The people then realized that small grants were not sufficient to deal with their level of deprivation and poverty. Any project not controlled by the people themselves, furthermore, only led them into dependency and was thus neither empowering nor developmental. In situations where certain initiatives were both important and necessary to the people, but they lacked control of the inputs, efforts were made to help the people gain control of these means of production before they began. Where this was not possible, the people went into a project knowing that it was likely to fail due to outside controlled inputs.

There was then a change of strategy from small-scale, income-generating activities to large employment-creating activities. Such activities were formulated to give service to a larger community while at the same time creating some employment.

Such activities as village markets, dam construction for improved irrigation schemes, cattle-fattening, grinding mills, village workshops in which tools and household equipment are made and repaired, and village "development centers" were initiated. These are so far doing very well, being not only self-sustaining but also making a financial contribution to the movement. Such initiatives pay for local salaries for the local training and educational programs, administrative costs of development centers and the overall financing of ORAP as a movement—including the transportation and hospitality costs incurred by those village representatives who attend the meetings.

It soon became apparent that as successful as some of these initiatives may have been, they tended to exclude and marginalize women and the very poor families in a given locality. Further changes were then made, this time not only in the strategy but also in the whole structure of ORAP. Previously, the ORAP structure began with a group of thirty to one hundred families who met for dialogue or around a specific activity, such as dam construction. Up to six such groups formed an "umbrella." At this level, larger issues were discussed and such projects as cattle-fattening were implemented. An unspecified number of "umbrellas" formed an association. Four representatives, two women and two men from each association, made up the Advisory Board, a policy and decision-making body. Board meetings were, however, open to any members from group or "umbrellas" should they wish to share any concerns, ideas or strategies with the Board.

After some concern was expressed that bigger projects tended to create class divisions within a community, the Board chose four of its members from four different villages in Matabeleland North/South and Midlands to undertake participatory action-research on the issue. All twelve ORAP associations were visited, with discussions on "development" and other related issues held at various levels of each association. The main objectives were to evaluate the effectiveness of the ORAP structure and programs in terms of whether or not they were benefiting or reaching poor families, to identify any obstacles and to encourage the people to make suggestions for any changes for the better.

Several suggestions emerged from this process. Here are four:

(1) If "development" is about people, then it must take place first in people's minds and where people are and not only at the project sites.

(2) The "development" agenda must be influenced by the people's needs and should be formulated by all those engaged in the process. Such an agenda must address itself directly to the people's everyday lives, how they live and how they want to change for the better.

(3) Developing one person in a family is not developmental, as her/his contributions to the whole family in cash or kind cannot be a substitute for the family's overall development.

(4) Any people-determined and people-controlled transformation cannot take place without a people's organizational base in which they freely and immediately implement what they have decided to do. Such an organizational base has to be rooted in the people's culture and their way of life.

In this exercise the people resolved that if ORAP as a movement is not to be diverted and thus serve the interest of a few, its structure, priorities and ways of work have to be based on the people's traditional organizational structures and needs. It was then suggested that the basis of ORAP structure should be the *amalima*—the traditional Ndebele family working units or groups. The spirit and philosophy of ORAP should thus be influenced directly by the ways of work of *amalima*.

Amalima are groups of five to ten family neighborhoods, which in traditional Ndebele come together to discuss, plan and implement ideas. Organized mainly around agricultural activities, clearing of land, ploughing, planting, weeding and harvesting, they were also effective in the construction of homes, granaries, cattle pens, improvement of community water supplies and so forth. All services are volunteered with the intention of helping one another improve their lot.

After this participatory research by the people for the people, three districts—Gwanda and Mzingwane (in Matabeleland South) and Silobela in the Midlands—immediately re-adopted the *amalima* concept, and within a year family-to-family solidarity in the form of strong human relationships, unity of purpose and concrete improvement in each family's quality of life became visible.

Consequently the ORAP structure now originates in *amalima* or family units. At this level, up to ten families meet to discuss and act together. In Gwanda forty-five such families identified some of their needs and problems as arising from the poverty that crippled dignity and health, and mobilized their own resources to reverse this situation. Activities included overall improvement of their homesteads, such as construction of toilets and kitchens, creating better educational conditions for their children and improved food production.

Dividing themselves into groups of five, families made contributions to the program according to each individual status. Those whose members were employed outside contributed cash, while those who were home-based contributed ideas and labor. For instance, after experimentation the women produced a certain type of soil which, when mixed with charred grain stocks and a type of leaf combined together in a certain way and in certain proportions, acted as a substitute for cement. This is used to plaster and polish their walls and floors, providing a smooth, hard heat- and water-resistant surface. The compound is also used to construct indoor fuel-saving stoves and ovens which, unlike those with a cement finish, do not crack even under constant high heat. Each woman designed her own kitchen while others helped put her ideas into effect, so although similar in many ways, each kitchen was unique.

As each kitchen was completed, cash was contributed to outfit them. Ten of each item needed by the women were purchased, including cups, plates, cutlery and a few pots and pans. With each delivery of these utensils, some cash was left to enable families to meet other needs. In this way educational expenses for their children were met.

During the growing season, families took turns in cultivating, planting and working one another's plots. A mugfull of seeds—whatever available of pumpkin, melons, beans, maize, small grains and other indigenous crops—was brought to be mixed together and planted. In this way the very poor families, who had lost their oxen and seeds in the drought years, received help and benefits they would otherwise never have had. In performing these daily agricultural rounds, some cash was also distributed to poorer families to help with any food needs as well as to replace any agricultural tools. Thus no one was left unable to produce their own food. Traditional methods of inter-cropping were shared and revived, and some of the indigenous seeds thought to be totally lost re-acquired.

This group of forty-five families then joined with another group to construct a dam. In previous years each of the family units had dug and protected wells, but these dried up in the drought years. With very little underground water, Gwanda was especially affected with severe food and water shortages. So a decision was taken to revert to dams. Although outside help was received in the form of a few bags of cement and technical advice from the government, all other inputs came from within the two communities. Good rains over 1987-88 found the communities well prepared. Every family produced enough food and more varieties than ever before, and their dam collected water to full capacity.

Families in the area continue to act together. Some future plans include a preschool, irrigation plots (watered from the dam) and improved food storage. And this evolutionary process is all from within.

Individuals from such family groups are increasingly being chosen to represent the people's interests at "umbrella," association and board levels. At all these levels, they exercise people's power to make decisions and to effect changes to their benefit. Today ORAP is one of the most effective indigenous people's organizations, the grassroots membership of which is often in direct contact with government.

This particular community has had, for example, protracted and difficult negotiations with the government over a piece of land that had been chosen as the site for their village development center. After making their choice and obtaining approval from one ministry, they began working on the land. But the Ministry of Roads then decided to run a road through the property. In the past the poor would have given in; the experts would have had their way without any resistance from the people.

In this case, however, delegations from the villages went to see the council and the district/provincial administrators. After some discussion, a meeting was convened in which the community delegation met with all top provincial government officials and the ministries concerned. It was suggested at one of the meetings that representatives from the village group and those from the relevant government ministries survey the site together. In the end, the road was diverted to pass through a different area and the community retained their land.

Conclusion

From the above example of ORAP, it can be concluded that people's power can best be regained from within and through participation. Rural people have their own perceptions of the world and how their future should be. Given the right kind of climate, the process of realizing these perceptions can be an empowering process.

The above examples also show that participation and the empowerment of people are not possible without an element of self-reliance in terms of attitude of mind, a strong organizational base and an ability to organize their own resources to improve their situation. On the other hand, self-reliance cannot be achieved through projects alone. People need first to engage in a participatory process.

Participation, self-reliance and people's empowerment are therefore inseparable. You cannot have one without the others and true advancement of all the people is not possible in a non-participatory society.

Chapter 9

TOWARD A KNOWLEDGE DEMOCRACY: VIEWPOINTS ON PARTICIPATORY RESEARCH IN NORTH AMERICA

John Gaventa

In an essay on research and education, Paulo Freire wrote: "If I perceive the reality as the dialectical relationship between subject and object, then I have to use methods for investigation which involve the people of the area being studied as researchers; they should take part in the investigation themselves and not serve as the passive objects of the study" (Freire 1982). With Freire's observation in mind, participatory research seeks to break down the distinction between the researchers and the researched and the subjects and objects of knowledge production through the participation of the people-for-themselves in the attainment and creation of knowledge. In the process, research is viewed not only as a means of creating knowledge; it is simultaneously a tool for the education and development of consciousness as well as mobilization for action.

Over the last ten years, a great deal of literature has developed around the theory and practice of participatory research. Much of it has its roots in Third World experiences, and has been labeled and promoted as a concept by persons involved in networks of adult education and development.

The participatory research method and idea are, however, by no means limited to the Third World. Within the U.S. and elsewhere in the First World, similar ideas have been developed, often originating from groups who, within their own context, share characteristics of domination by the knowledge system that are similar to those faced by their Third World counterparts. As such, participatory research may be observed in the following examples:

- In areas or by groups, where dominant knowledge has been a force for control but in which there is little access to sympathetic expertise. This includes such rural areas as Appalachia and oppressed groups whose interests are not well represented within the knowledge elite—minorities, women, workers, the poor. Lacking the capacity to rely on counter-experts for solutions to their problems, they must both create and struggle to attain knowledge on their own.

- Conducted by groups concerned with education of the people. Such groups may not be part of the formal adult education networks, which have often become highly professionalized and career-oriented, but consist of community groups, labor unions and minorities involved in concrete, grassroots-based action.

- Growing out of a concern for participation by the people in decisions that affect their lives, a theme that has been part of the New Left, civil rights, community organizing and environmental movements of the 1960s and 1970s.

Three strategies of popular participatory research have emerged that are particularly important in the North American context: (1) the reappropriation of knowledge, (2) development of knowledge and (3) participation in social production of knowledge.

The Reappropriation of Knowledge

Unlike many Third World countries, where information centers are almost entirely out of the reach of relatively powerless groups, in North America—the center of the information industry—there is potentially a vast storehouse of knowledge about peoples' lives. While abundant, such information is often beyond the ready access of those affected by it. Secrecy, privatization, professionalization or other characteristics of the knowledge society all shield it from ordinary people. Strategies to gain access to knowledge or reappropriate knowledge from the knowledge elite have been important ones for the citizen and worker-based research movement.

The approach draws heavily upon the investigative research tradition in the United States, and upon the public interest research movement championed by Ralph Nader. However, this approach not only popularizes information possessed by the knowledge elite but also the process of obtaining it. It insists that those who are directly affected by a problem have the right to acquire information about it for themselves.

There are numerous examples of this approach:

- *Community power structure research.* In many cases citizens have learned to research their own power structures through gaining access to courthouse records about property transactions, tax rates, housing codes, land and mineral ownership, government records about company finance, military industries and so forth. Popular manuals and training programs have taught groups to develop these skills for themselves.

- *Corporate research.* Vast quantities of information exist in the public sector about corporations which affect workers and communities in the U.S. and abroad. Other data exist in the hands of federal and state agencies that are supposed to regulate corporate behavior. While much of such research may be done for grassroots groups by sympathetic professionals, a number of good manuals exist on how workers and communities may obtain information themselves (for example, AFL-CIO 1984).

- *"Right-to-know" movements.* Workers, community groups

and professionals in a number of towns and states have launched campaigns which focus on the public's right to knowledge on the contents of toxic chemicals that are used at work or affect their communities. Such information, it is argued, should not be the sole province of either the corporation or of the medical and scientific profession (see Nelkin and Brown 1984).

At the heart of these movements lies the basic claim for public access to information produced by the knowledge system. Compared to citizens' research in other countries, groups are vastly aided by the Freedom of Information Act, which provides citizens access to an array of government documents possibly affecting the public interest. Many states have also passed similar legislation. The effective use of the FOIA by groups, and the popularization of it, has resulted in an attempt to weaken existing legislation, especially in the Reagan administration, and to invoke such arguments as "national security" in order to keep the information from the public.

In our work at the Highlander Center, we have found that this process of people gaining control over knowledge and skills, normally considered to be the monopoly of the experts, is an empowering one that produces much more than just the information in question.

While many action groups have considered research as an antecedent to action, to be done by the researcher and then passed on to the group, this approach to research can be viewed as a means of popular action in itself. To the extent that power has been exercised through the control of knowledge, then people may confront the power structure through regaining that knowledge or its tools for themselves. Those who successfully do so experience the thrill and excitement of regaining for themselves what previously had been the property of the expert.

The participatory process used in confronting the knowledge holders also provides an opportunity to develop a consciousness on how the power structure actually works. People may discover for themselves dominant knowledge or interpretations of reality which do not confirm their own experience—in which case they must ask, why not? Or the process of popular investigation may reveal previously hidden information that does confirm through "official" knowledge what the people have suspected from their own experience. When the former occurs, people may continue to question and to pursue the contradictions. When the latter is the case, the fusion of the official knowledge with that of popular experience lends validity to the peoples' claims and may unleash new action, as in the case of the black lung movement in West Virginia. In that instance, Drs. Rassmussen, Buff and others in the medical profession "revealed" to the miners that they were "right" in suspecting that breathing problems really came from the mines, and not from inherent asthma as doctors had previously claimed (Derickson 1983).

Within this context, the idea of literacy assumes new meaning. Historical experience in literacy programs shows that "literacy from the top" is not particularly effective in helping people learn to read, nor in altering their position within society. In fact, it may simply be a way to extend to the illiterate the skills needed by the dominant society. On the other hand, when the process of becoming literate is tied to a process of struggle, of gaining knowledge for action, it becomes a far more successful experience, both in the skills that people learn and the consciousness they develop about the society as a whole.

Similarly, today, literacy may take the form of those disenfranchised by the knowledge system learning new knowledge or skills, the lack of which excludes them from participation in decision making in their own lives. At Highlander, for example, we have taught those with a low level of education how to read medical textbooks in order to understand for themselves whether chemicals in their water or workplace are destroying their health. Others have taught workers how to understand corporate accounts, complex legal records or how to use computers. Motivated to gain knowledge for themselves, the disenfranchised have an enormous capacity to acquire skills and knowledge normally considered the province of the expert.

Once people begin to view themselves as researchers—that is, able to investigate reality for themselves—they will develop other popular and indigenous ways of gaining information from the power structure—what we have come to label "guerilla research." Coal miners, needing data on their employer, have discovered a great deal of useful information by monitoring garbage cans at corporate headquarters. Alliances may develop within the plant among the secretaries in the manager's office and among the workers. Workers on the production line may remove the labels from chemicals barrels to research in medical textbooks. Or they may persuade company laboratory workers to run tests on the sly in an effort to discover what the real impact on their health might be. Workers and grassroots activists have learned to use their own water sampling kits, video cameras and computers to compile needed information. Because those who are experiencing the problem also become the ones researching it, there will be available a variety of community-based approaches and information sources open to them not accessible to the outside professional.

Now armed with the information, several things may happen. First, the process of confronting the experts and gaining an understanding of their tools and their knowledge may serve to demystify the myth of expertise itself. People may learn that the"scientific" foundation upon which regulations are made, and through which their own experiences are discounted, are not so solid, that they are subject to fallibility, conflicting viewpoints, misinterpretation and plain falsification. With this revelation also comes a renewed examination of their own "popular knowledge," which they have been taught to deprecate since their first days of schooling. Attitudes of dependency begin to move toward ones of self-reliance.

Second, those who participate in the unmasking of dominant knowledge and the exposure of the power structure now "own" the knowledge they have gained and can reflect upon it.

Finally, the process becomes a resource for analyzing the dominant ideas, or it may help to clarify strategies through the identification of the Achilles' heel of the system where action should begin.

While the process of reappropriation of dominant knowledge by those who are affected by it is empowering as a strategy, by itself it is limited. Although participatory, it is still based upon gaining access to and control over knowledge that has already been codified by others. It is an access to a paradigm which the people had little part in creating. A further strategy evolves as the powerless develop, create and systematize their own knowledge and begin to define their own science.

Developing the Peoples' Knowledge

The intellectual roots for the peoples' science concept are

developed quite forcefully in the participatory research literature, most clearly by Orlando Fals-Borda: "We regard popular
science—folklore, popular knowledge or popular wisdom—to
be the empirical or common sense knowledge belonging to the
people at the grassroots and constituting part of their cultural
heritage." Such knowledge is not usually codified but is the
"practical, vital and empowering knowledge which has allowed
them to survive, interpret, create, produce and work over the
centuries [and] has its own rationality and causality structure."
It "remains outside the formal scientific structure built by the intellectual minority of the dominant system because it involves a
breach of the rules, and hence its subversive potential" (Fals-
Borda 1982). The ideas also draw upon the European Gramscian
tradition, which considers the capacity of every person to be an
intellectual, and to develop a popular, organic knowledge that
converts spontaneous common sense into "good sense."

Much of the writing about popular knowledge places great
value on that knowledge which grows directly out of nature
(from a peasant-based culture) and pits it against the dominant
knowledge of the industrialized world. The knowledge of folk
medicine, peasant technology or means of survival are all examples of useful knowledge, the validity of which has been suppressed by Western science and Western technology. The book
by Robert Chambers, *Rural Development: Putting the Last First*
(1983), describes and documents many instances in which the
knowledge of "primitive," pre-industrialized peoples proved
more useful and appropriate to them than did that of the modernization agents. Such knowledge, it is argued by Fals-Borda,
must be recovered through oral histories and other research, systematized and preserved to provide a power to resist Western in-
dustrialization, and to chart a more authentic future.

Given the emphasis on peoples' knowledge as peasant
knowledge, some writers in the participatory research debate
have asked, "Is it a concept useful for participatory research
within the industrialized and even post-industrialized Western
world?" We must answer "Yes." The experiences of Appalachia,
blacks, native Americans, ethnic minorities and others
demonstrate the existence of cultures in which knowledge has
not been fully absorbed by the dominant knowledge structures.

What, though, of the oppressed groups in our society who
can lay no claim to a "folk" or "peasant" past, who are in some

sense a product themselves of the industrial world and of Western science? Do they possess a popular knowledge? Again, we argue "Yes." It must be remembered that Gramsci's ideas, which are often used in reference to the notion of popular knowledge, grew not out of the context of a peasant economy vs. an industrialized one, but out of his experiences with the Italian workers' struggle in which the value of the workers' own knowledge was diminished by the hegemony of the ruling class. Within the Western world, popular knowledge is constantly being created in the daily experiences of work and community life. The legitimacy of such knowledge, too, is constantly being devalued and suppressed by the dominant science.

Within industrial and post-industrial societies, as within peasant societies, popular production and recovery of the common persons' knowledge is also a means of gaining strength. There are many examples:

- Popular planning of new communities and workplaces draws upon peoples' knowledge, and visions for the future. One of the most significant examples of such planning was that of the Lucas Aerospace Workers in Britain, who, when faced with closure of their industry, developed their own ideas of new, socially useful products to manufacture. (Wainwright and Elliott 1982).

- Peoples' health surveys have allowed the systematization of their own experiences with environmental and occupational problems. The power of this approach as a mobilizing and knowledge production tool has been seen, for example, in Rocky Flats, Colorado, leading to an organized protest against nuclear poisoning, and in Love Canal, resulting in a campaign to clean up toxic waste dumps. In both cases the "discovery" of devastating health problems came not by the scientists but from "housewife researchers," who were led by their own experiences to document and analyze the health experiences of others in the community (see Levine 1982).

- The workers' history movement, sparked in part by Sven Lindquist's book *Dig Where You Stand* (1982) in Sweden, has encouraged workers to use their own knowledge to develop their own history as well as other methods to reclaim the corporate and "official" versions of their facts.

As in the case of reclaiming knowledge from the dominant system, this process of popular production of the peoples' knowledge has a number of effects upon its participants. Seeing themselves capable of producing and defining their own reality they may actively seek to change it, a greater consciousness and analysis of the political context and of their situation may develop and the new knowledge becomes a resource for challenging the hegemony of the dominant ideas.

However, this approach also has its limitations. To the extent that it relies upon the peoples' experience as the basis of knowledge, how does it develop knowledge within the people that may be in their interest to know but is outside of their experience? What about the situation in which neither the dominant knowledge production system nor the peoples' own knowledge have the information to respond to the potential impact of a new technological development, such as the introduction of a new chemical in the workplace? Are there not circumstances, even for the oppressed, in which there is a need for a science which is democratic, but which does not require all of the people to become scientists in order to control and benefit from it? Is direct participation in all aspects of the knowledge production system the only form of its popular control? Is there not some need for a division of labor, which recognizes that it is more useful for certain persons to act as researchers and others to act as controllers of their own destiny in other ways?

Popular Participation in the Social Production of Knowledge

Obviously the only response to expert domination is not to clone the expert in every person, or even in every oppressed group. The alternative involves forms of democratic participation and control in defining the problems to be studied, in setting research priorities and in determining how the results are to be used. It means recognizing the importance of the production of scientific knowledge by scientists as one type of knowledge production that is not inherently superior to others. Such strategies would insist, as some have proposed, on having lay persons involved in deciding about the production of knowledge, if not actually doing it, i.e., through the development of popularly controlled research centers.

In actual practice, examples of this approach are less developed in North America than are the emerging approaches for popular reappropriation of knowledge, or for developing the peoples' science. Elements of the approach are found in some research groups in Denmark and Sweden, where "reference groups" of those affected by research are involved with professional researchers in carrying out projects. In the Utopia Project members of the Typographical Workers Union work side by side with professional researchers to analyze the impact of new technology upon their workplaces. Other elements of this strategy are found as relatively powerless groups demand a voice in allocation of public research funds, as was found in the Appalachian Land Ownership Study (Gaventa and Horton 1981).

Such models demand new forms of accountability. While scientists and experts may conduct research for the people, it is very different from that which originates when the professional in the knowledge system defines what knowledge should be provided to the people, or when the committed intellectual seeks to build awareness through research with the people. In a situation where the people have become active, self-conscious of their own knowledge and aware of the limitations of the experts' knowledge (that is, when they have thrown off knowledge-based domination by the experts), then they can also participate fully in decisions about the production of new knowledge, for themselves and for society. The domination arising from the "people-as-objects" of research is transformed to the "people-as-subjects," determining the directions of scientific and theoretical inquiry.

Some Implications: Toward a Knowledge Democracy

In recent years there has been much debate about the need for an economic democracy, which suggests that the control and concentration of economic production in the hands of a few must be altered if we are to realize a real political democracy. The concentration of dominating knowledge in the hands of the few and the power to proclaim it as "official" is also producing new debates about what constitutes genuine democracy in a knowledge society. In their conservative neo-elitist forms, the argument is for greater government by expertise, and against the "irrationality" of participation by the masses in the knowledge production system. In their liberal form these arguments are for greater access and more equal opportunity for all members of the public to benefits of the existing knowledge system and paradigms. But in their most radical form these arguments recognize that it is not enough simply to democratize access to existing information. Rather, fundamental questions must be raised about what knowledge is produced, by whom, for whose interests and toward what end. Such arguments begin to demand the creation of an alternative organization of science—one that is not only *for* the people but is created *with* them and *by* them as well.

Genuine popular participation in the production of knowledge has implications, of course, not only for the realization of classical notions of democracy but also for the body of knowledge that is to be produced. By altering who controls knowledge, the type of knowledge produced—and, indeed, the very definition of what constitutes knowledge—may also change. For example, given a chance to participate in the production of knowledge about products, not simply in their production, the Lucas workers chose to develop plans that met basic social needs and not those that served as instruments of war. Given the opportunity to define the reasons for poverty through self-analysis, the participants in the Appalachian Land Ownership Study gave a very different set of reasons than those developed by the mainstream social scientists. The believer in popular participation must hope that the vision and view of the world that is produced by the many will be more humane, rational and liberating than the dominating knowledge of today that is generated by the few.

PART III

STEPS IN PRAXIOLOGY

Chapter 10

STIMULATION OF SELF-RELIANT INITIATIVES BY SENSITIZED AGENTS: SOME LESSONS FROM PRACTICE

S. Tilakaratna

Grassroots experiences from many developing countries have demonstrated that the spirit of self-reliance, which often lies dormant in people who live in poverty and deprivation, can be activated by appropriate stimulation using sensitized agents. With such stimulation, the people concerned tend to take collective initiatives—creative and assertive actions—to improve their socio-economic-cultural status. This chapter summarizes lessons derived from four aspects of such self-reliant development experiences, namely: (1) the nature and mode of stimulation, (2) the process by which sensitized agents have been created to play such a role, (3) the different kinds of self-reliant actions that people have initiated following such stimulation, and finally (4) the issue of sustaining such initiatives on a broader front. The discussion is based primarily on experiences in South and Southeast Asia.[1]

The Nature and Mode of Stimulation

Stimulation of the poor and deprived to undertake self-reliant initiatives requires two essential steps.

The first is the development of an awareness about the reality in which they live. In particular, they need to understand that poverty and deprivation are a result of specific social forces rather than an outcome of some inherent deficiency on their part or even "fate." Second, based on such critical awareness, they need to gain confidence in their collective abilities to bring about positive changes in their life situations and to organize themselves for that purpose.

A stimulation of this sort implies a specific mode of interaction with the people, the essence of which could be summarized as the breaking up of the classical dichotomy between "subject" and "object" (manipulation and dominance) and its replacement by a humanistic mode of equal relation between two subjects (animation and facilitation). Such a mode of interaction would be fundamentally different from that adopted by a political party worker or a conventional development worker. The essential differences may be summarized as follows:

- Starting from where people are—their experiences, knowledge, perceptions and rhythm of work and thought (rather than from a preconceived political agenda or an externally conceived set of assumptions).

- Stimulating the people (animation) to undertake self-analysis of their life situations (a self-inquiry into the economic-social-cultural environment in which people live) and helping them derive from such self-inquiry facts, figures and conclusions to serve as an intellectual base for initiating changes (rather than the use of a closed framework of analysis or a social analysis carried out by outside intellectuals).

- Assisting the people to organize themselves and to create their own organizations—People's Organizations (POs)—

which are non-hierarchical in structure and democratic in operations and which can effectively be used as instruments of action to create change (rather than organizing people into externally determined structures to serve goals set by outsiders).

- Facilitating the actions for change as decided by the POs, in particular assisting them to deal with logistical and practical problems which the people by themselves may not initially be fully equipped to cope with (rather than implementation of externally conceived projects/programs).

- Stimulating and assisting the POs to carry out self-reviews of their activities as a regular practice, to assess and learn from successes as well as failures and to plan future actions (rather than monitoring and evaluation carried out by outsiders).

- Conscious measures taken by the external agent to make his/her role progressively redundant in order to pave the way for and thus ensure self-reliant capacity buildup of the POs (rather than attempting to provide continued leadership and patronage or to project one's image).

- Such a phasing out would necessarily require assistance in developing their own cadres (internal animators and facilitators) who could eventually replace the external agents. Moreover, selected internal animators/facilitators will be used for the expansion of the self-reliant development process (to cover new villages/communities), thereby reducing the dependence on external agents as well as the cost of external animation (rather than the use of a large number of external agents, which is costly and often requires high recourse to foreign funds).

Creation of a Cadre of Sensitized Agents

Adoption of a mode of interaction with the people as described above requires the availability of a cadre of sensitized agents who have gone through a process of rigorous learning based on exposure to concrete experiences and self-reflection, as against formal training and instruction. Analysis of several country experiences reveal that potential persons have originated from (1) socially conscious and active segments of the middle class who have had some practical experience in social activities, have gone through secondary or higher formal education and are generally in the age category of twenty-five to forty; and (2) those who had begun to critically reflect on whatever activist roles they had been playing earlier and were looking for more relevant or fulfilling roles in society.[2]

The learning process undergone to develop potential should be distinguished from formal training courses where the trainee becomes an object of training and a depository of knowledge delivered by a trainer. The main elements of the learning process as revealed from practice may be summarized as follows:

- The starting point is a collective reflection on and an analysis of the experiences that "trainees" already have in working with communities and their existing knowledge of micro and macro social situations. Such a critical review of existing knowledge and experiences provides an opportunity for each "trainee" to engage in self-criticism and self-evaluation, to initiate a process of "unlearning" as well as new learning.

- Beginning from such an initial self-reflective exercise, the trainees are exposed to concrete field situations by living among selected communities in order to gather socio-economic information through informal discussions with the people and through direct observations as a base for understanding community life.

- Such an exercise in basic data gathering enables the trainee to identify those categories of the poor and deprived. Through interaction with such groups, the trainee seeks to stimulate them to identify issues of common concern, collect the relevant data on these issues and assist them in analyzing the data that will enrich an understanding of their own life situations. It requires a sustained effort on the part of a trainee to be able to set in motion such a process of self-inquiry by the people.

- While engaged in such field exercises, the trainees meet regularly (at least once a month) as a group to share and analyze their experiences among themselves as a collective learning exercise. This transference from field action to collective reflection is an important method for the trainees to improve the quality of their work by learning from each other's experiences.

- While there can be no definitive time table, concrete experiences suggest that trainees generally take at least six months to achieve a breakthrough in learning and action, that is, to acquire the basic skills for stimulation and demonstrate some concrete results in the field. At this point, the trainees would begin to show varying degrees of success in stimulating the people, with whom they had been interacting, to organize themselves so to initiate changes. The progress is not necessarily even; some would lag behind others.

- As an important part of these field exercises, the trainees also should identify these individuals from within the communities that possess the potential skills in animation and facilitation, and should assist in improving such skills. Creation of internal or community cadres is an important requirement for the ultimate phasing out of the external cadres.

Thus it is seen that the creation of sensitized agents is a process that involves sustained field experiences coupled with back-and-forth exercises for collective learning spread over a number of months. It is a delicate human resource development that cannot be short-circuited or capsuled into a short-term training course to be delivered in a class room.

Given their formal education and middle-class origin and aspirations, the external animators tend to go through many tensions in their work with the people, for example, comparisons with peer groups, middle-class lifestyles, demands of the family and careerist tendencies. These factors make it difficult to retain many of the external animators for long, resulting in a high turnover. Experience shows that after about four to five years of work, a sense of fatigue sets in, at which point many of them seek job change. Moreover, since they have to be paid salaries and allowances at least comparable to going market rates, their use in large numbers is a costly matter. This would lead to overextended budgets often requiring increased dependence on foreign donors.

In order to avoid both a high dependence on external funds as well as the problems created by high turnover, it is necessary to confine the cadre of external animators to a modest number of carefully selected committed persons. This would invariably mean that Self-reliance Promoting Organizations (SPOs) will need to depend increasingly on selected internal animators (cadres of POs) to expand the process of self-reliant development and to increase its coverage geographically.

While some internal animators would be confined to the activities of their own POs, there would be others willing to cross the village boundaries to spread the development process in adjacent areas. Such persons may be labeled as Internal-External Animators, (IEAs), as distinguished from the external ones of the SPOs and internal ones of the POs. They represent an intermediate category, being those from among the cadres of a PO willing to undertake external animation by going beyond the boundary of the respective PO. The use of their services on a part-time basis would require only a payment of a replacement income (alternative daily income foregone plus travel cost) which would greatly reduce the cost of external animation.[3]

Emergence of Self-reliant Actions

Sparked by the stimulation provided by sensitized agents, the kinds of actions that organized groups of people have initiated vary depending on the particular socio-economic-cultural context—that is, the nature and extent of the deprivations, concerns of the people and the availability of political and social space for desired actions. The diverse variety of actions that have emerged may be analyzed under four interrelated types, namely, defensive, assertive, constructive and innovative/alternative actions.

Defensive actions by the poor are basically aimed at protecting the existing sources, means and levels of living against erosion or encroachment by the actions of other interest groups or by governmental policies or projects. Examples are dislocations and displacements of people and loss of their customary means of living as a result of such "development projects" as big dams for electricity generation of agribusiness operations. Other examples include adverse effects of the introduction of big trawlers on small fishermen, environmental damage caused by some projects or certain so-called development policies. Actions by organized groups have taken a variety of forms, such as protest campaigns, making representations to public authorities, negotiations for compensation, resort to legal remedies and other direct actions.

Assertive actions refer to assertions by the poor deprived of economic, social and other rights available to them under governmental legislation, policies and programs as well as what they collectively consider to be their legitimate entitlements. Experiences show that governmental legislation and policies intended to benefit the poor and deprived—e.g., rights of sharecroppers and tenants, minimum wages, delivery schemes and poverty programs—do not automatically reach the poor unless the latter are organized and able to act as a pressure group to assert their rights. Through organizations of their own making, the poor have enhanced their receiving capacity as well as their claim-making capacity for such rights and public services. Assertive action has a further dimension: assertion vis-à-vis private vested interests that attempt to make extractions from the poor through a process of unequal or unfair exchange—exorbitant interest charged on credit supplies, low prices paid for peasant produce or high prices charged for inputs used by peasants. In social contexts where such income transfers (from poor to rich) are an important factor in the poverty of the peasantry, organized peasant groups have initiated collective actions to enhance their bargaining power as opposed to mercantile or landed interests. Or they have delinked from them, initiating alternative (cooperative) methods of credit and marketing arrangements and thereby retrieving formerly lost economic surpluses.

Constructive actions refer to projects of a self-help nature initiated by organized groups to satisfy the group needs by mobilizing their own resources and skills with or without supplementary assistance from outside. Such activities could take a variety of forms: (1) infrastructural works—feeder roads, simple irrigation works and similar physical structures; (2) economic projects, such as consumer good stores, schemes for credit and marketing and small industries; (3) social development projects, such as drinking water wells, housing improvements and health and education programs; and (4) cultural activities of different sorts.

Finally, *innovative or alternative actions* represent initiatives of organized groups to experiment with and undertake development styles and activities that could be alternatives to some elements of the mainstream "development" processes. These may be technologies that are ecologically sustainable and more appropriate to the environment and culture of the people. Organic farming, biogas projects and indigenous practices of health care are examples. Recovery and revival of indigenous cultural elements that suffered under cultural invasions is a further dimension. Evolution of innovative organizational forms and methods of community action that are democratic and participatory in character, and also capable of checking the growth of elitist forms of leadership within organizations, represent another example.

Issues in the Sustainability of Self-reliant Processes

Experiences vary as to the extent the above-described actions have proved self-sustaining or have led to a continuing improvement in the socioeconomic status of the poor and deprived. While some have shown more durable results, others have stagnated, lacked continuity or failed to develop after an initial spurt of activity. Analysis of concrete experiences reveal that the sustainability of organized initiatives appears to depend on four interrelated factors: (1) the emergence of a group of internal animators, (2) practice of self-review by people's organizations, (3) the ability to move from micro groups to larger groupings, and finally (4) an expansion of the action agenda to move toward a total/comprehensive development effort.

The first important development must be the emergence of a group of internal (community) cadres who possess the skills to animate their fellow men and women, to facilitate the group actions (and thus multiply the development beyond village boundaries) and to progressively reduce the dependence on external cadres. External cadres, who tend to persist without the creation of internal cadres, consciously or unconsciously create a new form of dependency among the people. This is particularly the case when such external cadres also function as some sort of delivery agents, for example, for credit and other inputs.

A progressive increase in the ratio of internal animators to a given external agent is in fact an important indicator of capacity buildup for self-reliance. As we have already observed, the existence of a pool of internal animators becomes an important source of internal-external animators, thus reducing the cost of external animation.

Second, for the emergence of a viable people's process, self-review of activities must become a regular practice of people's organizations. Self-review is an action-reflection process which evaluates the ongoing actions by the people themselves, enabling any corrections or adjustments therein as well as providing a base for the conception and planning of future actions. Moreover, it is an important instrument of assertion vis-à-vis outsiders (including the external animator) as well as their own leaders. Self-review needs to include not only the people's actions, but also their relations with outsiders as well as relations among themselves. In short, self-review helps to improve people's actions, assert their autonomy and create conditions for the democratic functioning of people's organizations.

Third, the process of development that initially emerges is rooted in small-sized base groups that often encompass members having common interests or are subject to similar disabilities. There are many actions that such small groups can take by themselves to improve conditions. But a point is reached when the feasible agenda for autonomous actions becomes exhausted and stagnation tends to set in. Hence the continued ability of such organized entities to make advances depends on their ability to forge links with one another and to evolve into larger organizations through appropriate groupings with the objective of expanding the available space for actions. This is the only way by which organized groups are able to move on to a higher plane of action and thus open up even newer possibilities for action. In order to tackle larger issues of common concern, which are beyond the capacity of any single group acting alone to deal with, there is a need to grow bigger, to enhance bargaining power and to emerge as a power to reckon with within a given social context. This tends to be an organic development in the case of groups that have attained a relatively high level of consciousness through an action-reflection process. Such groups are actively seeking ways to expand the space for assertive and creative actions. Broader groupings emerge as a logical necessity, a felt need. When group formations on a broader front fail to emerge, micro-level initiatives (after a point) tend to stagnate and even fizzle out or become coopted into the ongoing mainstream.

And finally, there is the need to broaden and deepen the action agenda by progressively moving from initial issues of concern to a total development effort—an integrated advance on several fronts which could make a significant impact on the life situations of the people concerned. The initial actions may be, for example, defensive or assertive ones (as described above), which should then be followed by constructive and innovative actions in order to create a base for continuing life improvements. With the formation of larger groupings/organizations in a given geographical area, a sizeable base would be available to facilitate the formulation of comprehensive plans that could stand as alternatives to the mainstream "development" activities and programs. Such alternative development plans, based as they are on visions, values, priorities and aspirations of conscientized groups, could be used as instruments for bargaining with governments or public agencies for a legitimate share of resource allocation. In this way organized groups need to progressively advance to a stage where local/regional planning for a total development effort, embracing economic-social-cultural dimensions, could be initiated. In this final analysis the ability of participatory initiatives to multiply, expand and grow in the face of overwhelming pressures emanating from the mainstream—dependence, alienation, atomization, consumerism and environmental destruction—will depend on the proven successes in developing innovations and alternative methods, practices, ideas and plans capable of making a significant improvement in the life situations of the poor on a continuing basis.

NOTES

1. For reports on some of these experiences, see Rahman 1984 and Tilakaratna 1985.
2. For some Asian experiences of the emergence of external animators, see Tilakaratna 1987.
3. The term SPO (Self-reliance Promoting Organizations), as distinguished from NGO, was adopted by the participants of a workshop in the Philippines to provide a separate identity for those organizations that specifically use a process as described in this chapter. The term Internal-External Animator (IEA) was also developed in this workshop

(Regional Workshop for Trainors in Participatory Rural Development, Tagaytay, The Philippines, August 1988).

Chapter 11

REMAKING KNOWLEDGE

Orlando Fals-Borda

Building up people's self-awareness has been an ever-present preoccupation of participatory action researchers—an extremely important task in order for our actions to be effective if we want to avoid the betrayal of ideals. For this purpose, we have placed the interplay between explicit and implicit science—or between Cartesian and popular knowledge—in a practical and teletic context, as a fact which has to be taken into account since it involves dialectical encounters that are inevitably part of day-to-day living. In the course of our work on the five continents, as described in the previous chapters, we have seen enormous possibilities of combining the two types of knowledge, and doing so without tilting the balance in favor of academic knowledge monopolized mostly for exploitative purposes. Our central aim has been to direct this interplay to allow the common people to have sufficient control over the generation of new knowledge. We have therefore tried to encourage the remaking of knowledge and science for the benefit of the masses victimized by power.

We are, of course, too small for this tremendous task: the victims of poverty constitute the majority of the earth's inhabitants and the effort has many detractors. But a hopeful methodological start has been made with participatory action-research, as described at length in this book.

Certainly PAR has more supporters now than at the beginning, when theory was considered irrelevant or received low priority. A return to and refocusing of concepts, definitions and systematization soon became unavoidable as greater emphasis was put on clarity in verbal communication in the training of cadres—a setback for those who insisted on a radical break with the past as a condition for our new adventures. At the beginning, we had to use some well-worn categories and theories (class, state, dialectics) as well as cite a few authorities to launch our innovative attempts, although care was taken not to return to functionalist or positivist frames of reference. A reading of diverse fields and schools of thought had to be undertaken during those breathing spells allowed by the spiral of the action-reflection cycle.

It finally dawned on us that some of our fresh ways of looking at issues had antecedents which could have provided certainties for our fieldwork had they been considered before. What we were discovering was not, after all, entirely original. In many instances we were observing old phenomena under a new light as though looking at the flip-side of a coin.

The Positive Role of Subversion

Almost without knowing it, we immersed ourselves during the first years in some of the counter-currents of science described in 1978 by Nowotny and others who just skirted the risky and dangerous issue of institutional subversion. While these European colleagues were able to avoid being accused of subversion, those of us in the Third World experimenting with PAR soon came under official suspicion. We had to face the charge of subversion head on and early in the game. Some of us devised and proposed an anti-value with which to defend ourselves that we called "moral subversion." Now incorporated in some respected academic encyclopedias (cf. Del Campo 1976, II: 961-964), this "concept in reverse" induced some hesitation among the enemies of people's struggles and disarmed them ideologically and morally.

The needed archaeology of the concept of subversion took us back to the historical moment when it was invented by Sallust to refer to the Catilinian conspiracy in Rome (62 B.C.). Indeed, we learn from Sallust that it was Cicero and not Catiline, the leader of a slave and workers' revolt against corrupt senators, who was the immoral subversive. This, together with other historical and contemporary cases like those of Gandhi, Father Camilo Torres and Ernesto Che Guevara as well as the accounts of so many heretics and subverters who were subsequently rehabilitated as heroes or saints, led us to redefine subversion more realistically. We saw it as merely a condition reflecting the internal contradictions of a social order discovered in a given historical period under the light of new goals and values (Fals-Borda 1970).

This kind of positive subversion applied in the search for insights and more effective action eventually gave birth to new currents of thought in the Third World. One was the theology of liberation that gives inspiration to the important work of Christian-based communities. Others gave ideological support to work within institutions whenever they allow for a margin of tolerance for change (see Chapter 9, Gaventa's "guerilla research"). Innovations could then be introduced without much frontal resistance, as described in this book by Salazar (1987) in the case of the Colombian Ministry of Labour.

The Meaning of Dialogical Research

In adopting such marginal and subversive roles in practice, PAR researchers were not denying the merits of science; without the scientific bearings they would have felt as if moving in a void. In our new ventures we looked unconsciously for ways of building connections between the different scientific traditions while doing research with and for the people, and not on them. We could do this as activists and researchers by trying to combine both roles, a task for which we had received practically no training. It was impossible for those of us with formal schooling to forget all the lessons learned in academic halls; in fact, we made good use of such basic rules as applying rigor and responsibility in observation-inference or in the careful handling of data, just as positivists do. But we had to remake other aspects of our scholarship so as to relate it to ordinary people's way of interpreting reality and their common sense. In a similar manner we had to discover and apply their half-hidden science—their own "people's knowledge"—for their own benefit.

For this purpose, we developed a series of field procedures in which theory and practice, conventional learning and implicit knowledge could be combined in special *vivencias*. These procedures, sometimes called "synergistic" for their joint action implications (Zamosc 1987: 24-25), are still applied (de Roux has described it in Chapter 4) but are not binding. Imitation or replication of techniques is not recommended, not even when they have proved successful. The rules of cultural consistency make it preferable to undertake new actions every time, depending on the specific conditions and circumstances of each experience. Freedom to explore and to recreate in these conditions is therefore another essential characteristic of participatory action-research.

The reconstruction of knowledge for the purpose of furthering social progress and increasing people's self-awareness with PAR *vivencias* takes dialogue as its point of insertion in the social process. This is amply documented in Part II. It is dialogical research, oriented to the social situation in which people live, attempting to organize them and to break up the subject/object binomial. As actual situations in Third World societies (and probably elsewhere) generally involve capitalist exploitation, *vivencia* experiences start by asking base groups such questions as: "Why is there poverty?" or "Why is there oppression and dependence?" The answers may provide a greater awareness of their problems, and at the same time make them realize the need for finding out the reasons and taking political action.

Ideally in such cases as those described by Nyoni, Tilakaratna and Rahman, the grassroots representatives and cadres should be able to participate as reference groups in the action-research process from the very beginning—that is, from the moment it is decided what the subject of the research will be. And they should remain involved at every step of the process until the results (of which they continue to be rightful owners) have been published and the information has been returned in various ways to the people.

As shown in the preceding chapters, PAR gives precedence to qualitative rather than to quantitative analyses without losing sight of the importance of rigorous research and the applicability of other explanatory schemas. In this connection participatory researchers like de Roux have faced the unusual dilemma of employing affective logic involving sentiments and emotions versus dialectical logic with cold-headed analyses. As a rule, we have followed Pascal's dictum in his *Thoughts*: "The heart has its *reasons* which reason itself does not at all perceive," much as in biologist William Bateson's ideal that scientific work can reach its highest point when it aspires to art. If emotion and reason have their own algorithms, the discovery of these is not beyond human effort, as has been shown in the case of musical logic, for example, and by men of letters and aesthetes who have been able "to think with the heart." This unorthodox, infrequent combination has nevertheless been recognized by respected scholars as possible in the pursuit of science.

Autonomy and Collective Research

Following these general orientations, one of our first corroborations was the objective centrality of local know-how and autonomous experience, an obvious fact often obscured in regular academic training where we are told instead to despise and mistrust common sense and folk knowledge. The resulting cultural shock has been highly instructive for us. To begin with, as the testimonies in this book have shown, popular knowledge does not come in the form of isolated facts known to specific individuals. It comes in packets of cultural data generated by social groups. In PAR the information can be immediately processed, confronted and verified by motivated and fully aware participants. They have been found to perform better as a group—in meetings, committees, round tables, assemblies, debates, collective trips and so forth, as seen in Cauca, Ayacucho, Senegal, Tanzania, Zimbabwe and Appalachia. PAR as an autonomous collective investigation is quite different from the type of research usually recommended, where the (detached) observer takes the initiative and sole responsibility for the work with other purposes in mind—doctoral thesis, advancement of science, promotion, personal prestige or financial gain. Now the task becomes a communal enterprise in which social validation of knowledge is obtained not only by confronting previous ideas or hypotheses but also through the people's own verification mechanisms. This has been underlined by Rahman.

There are three theoretical elements—not usually included in dominant paradigms—which enrich the overall scientific experience in conducting and validating participatory action-research: (1) the ontological possibility of a real popular science, (2) the existential possibility of transforming the researcher/researched relationship, and (3) the essential need of autonomy and identity in exercising people's own countervailing power.

There is no need to elaborate on the well-known idea that the making of knowledge and science tends to favor those who produce and control them. They are not neutral nor value-free. And they can have many parents. In the field one can readily discern or conceive alternative functions of knowledge, such as a common people's science, as an endogenous process. People's science does exist in its explicit and implicit forms: it is formally constructed in its own terms, with its own practical rationality and empirical systematization and its own way of institutionalizing, accumulating and transmitting knowledge from one generation to the next. This science does not hinge on Cartesian or Kantian rationality. But it serves and should serve the interests of exploited classes (KSSP 1984; Guha 1988). This is especially true of health sciences ("folk medicine"), as outlined by Gaventa in Chapter 9.

What can students of social reality do with these hitherto neglected facts? They can establish, along with the contributors to this book, that the wisdom of the sage and the know-how of the scientist converge and intermingle, as recognized during their lifetimes by Descartes, Kant and Galileo themselves. Thus by giving due importance to both, contemporary students can help to produce a more useful and complete knowledge for social change, or "revolutionary science" in physicist Thomas Kuhn's terms (1962). Such convergence challenges the present positivist monopoly, the prophylactic and arrogant approach of academe, the ethnocentrism of Western science and dangerous technology. It therefore holds not only the richest of promises but also the greatest potential of both resistance and repression by vested interests.

Usually undaunted by such difficult prospects, participatory researchers approach their work with Antonio Gramsci's proposal in mind to convert common sense into "good sense." Emancipatory collective knowledge and popular science become tools in the quest for justice, and this is the answer to the perennial questions: "Knowledge for what?" and "Knowledge for whom?"

The second element, transformation of the researcher/researched (subject/object) liaison, brings us close to the contemporary debate on participation. This is certainly one of the concepts most used and abused since it was introduced by such liberal thinkers on egalitarian systems as J.J. Rousseau and J.S. Mill, or put in terms of equity by Adam Smith and other early economists (see Macpherson 1977: 93-115; Pateman 1970). PAR activists from the beginning have criticized the partial and interested definitions of participation given by Huntington (1976) and Vanek (1971). Since the Cartagena World Symposium on Action Research and Scientific Analysis in 1977, our concept is clearly centered on the idea that participation means more than support of government policy or the developmental passage from autocracy to representative democracy, as is commonly adduced (see Nyoni in Chapter 8). It means breaking up intentionally by means of *vivencias* the asymmetrical subject/object relationships of submission, dependence, exploitation and oppression that exist between persons, groups and social classes.

This interpretation has been substantiated by the cases dealt with in this book. Our definition of participation is more demanding. It is a teleological statement that sets up a standard to follow, one by which to measure social, economic and political advancement toward achievement of goals. In participatory action both researcher and researched recognize that despite their otherness they seek the mutual goal of advancing knowledge in search of greater justice. They interact, collaborate, discuss, reflect and report in collectivities on an equal footing, each one offering in the relationship what he knows best. For instance, outside cadres may provide technical expertise or situational analysis or act as intermediaries with other groups or institutions, while local cadres will provide specific local knowledge and know-how and by acting as critics will adapt the research to their own reality. It is in this space of a truly participatory activity that the actual meeting of diverse scientific traditions takes place, resulting in an enriched overall knowledge, which in addition is more effective in the struggle for justice and the achievement of social progress and peace.

In general terms, as recalled by Rahman, the breaking up of the initial subject/object binomial is problematic not only in the researcher-researched relationship but in all situations of daily life, from the family (macho structure) to education (*magister dixit*), health, material production, politics, military and ecclesiastical hierarchies, class structures and so forth. We, as activists, animators or agents of change, experience this difficulty as outsiders to the communities we work with when we look for local counterparts to be involved as reference groups. Given our differences of class and rationalities a tension is created between us. The resolution of this tension, as observed in the present cases, is obtained with the expression of mutual respect and a shared commitment, and through authentic collective participation in seeking new knowledge and synergistic experiences. These procedures, of course, overrun present academic rules and methods.

The third element—autonomy and identity in collective research—rests on the observation that progressive social movements and SPOs (Self-reliance Promoting Organizations) differ from other types of movements and regular institutional NGOs (see Tilakaratna in Chapter 10) in that they cherish and fight for their culture and personality to the last, and for good reason— their lives depend on it. A good PAR researcher recognizes the importance of this third characteristic and seeks to stimulate autonomous movements and to defend the articulation of local life as a worthy goal, not always shared by academe, governments and political parties (Kothari 1984; Restrepo 1988). As explained earlier by Gaventa, Nyoni, Gianotten and de Wit, the building up of autonomy is a delicate affair. It consists in stripping the oppressor of his power and in understanding how to internalize one's own. This is an effort in counter-alienation and in constructing "knowledge democracy," necessary for survival in the present ambiguous and violent contexts of many nations. It also includes the power to speak, since the cry of the poor for life and dignity is a condition *sine qua non* for any contemporary ethical stance (Clastres 1987: 151-155).

Hence the strong emphasis of participatory activists on undergirding the springs of social conduct by supporting self-reliant actions. This is done to defend human life and cultures; to improve self-management (autogestion); to build people's countervailing power, civic movements and self-reliance promoting organizations; and to provide a good margin for provincial, regional and civil-society actions vis-à-vis the state, central bureaucracies, monopolies, military complex and despotisms in general. The success or failure of these movements and organizations is one of the validation criteria in assessing the work of PAR researchers.[1]

This emphasis has produced several theoretical/practical consequences. One of them has been to reveal the dominant "discourse of development" for what it really is: an imposed model that perpetuates old distinctions between savage and civilized, and that works against the economy, autonomy and identity of our common people (Escobar 1987; Esteva 1987). This developmental model calls forth our subversive disaffection and criticism, to the horror of well-placed "establishment" experts, scientists and officials.

Our critical attitude toward the "development of under-development" in the Third World instigates alternative policies and authentic movements, such as those portrayed in Part II, for the application of technologies adapted to the common people's culture, needs and ends. In view of the debatable results of "green revolutions" and other developmentalist innovations, preference is given by PAR activists to work on knowledge systems for small-scale energy techniques and industries, and for reviving suitable practices in traditional agriculture and husbandry, housing, health care and other activities designed to defend poor and exploited communities. This is true even in the United States, as explained by Gaventa.

Of course, everyone knows that the autonomy and welfare of base groups, communities and regions, especially the most marginal and destitute, have diminished due to the forces of ill-conceived national integration, homogenization and "development" promoted by powerful central oligarchies (usually in imitation of European patterns of nation-states). This trend continues. Yet it is evident that even with all the repression and violence unleashed by the central states, they have not destroyed the core values and deep roots that sustain the communities and give them their culture and personality. The essays in this book confirm this. It has been one of PAR's important roles to rediscover with collective research the vitality of such values and roots, to stimulate positive, non-violent cultural contact and tolerance of different traditions and to foster movements of resistance and defense of local human, economic and political expressions (Sethi 1987). We have felt that there is still a deeply entrenched need for autonomy and cultural identity in regional, provincial and community life that simply needs stimulation in order to surface. This great effort can be the predicament of on-coming generations. If the eighteenth century in Europe has been called "the Enlightenment" for its collective efforts to revamp science and philosophy, the final decade of the 1990s and the twenty-first century may be expected to be the "Century of the Awakening." The common peoples are already awakening to their rights and possibilities for action in realizing these rights. They are also responding to the call of their own voices—hither-to half-muted—to honor their dignity and the meaning of their own history.[2]

Praxis and the Recovery of History and Culture

Official, elitist history has been *the* history for most social re-searchers because their formal training has often considered the common people's culture and daily life expressions second rate or not worthy of serious attention by scientists. This is no longer the case with participatory action-research and other methodologies (Heller 1984; Gleick 1987). We have recovered his-torical testimonies by scholars, acknowledging the popular, com-monsensical sources of their formulae. And we have dusted off memories of many simple people who have been prime movers of history but who, although as deserving as kings or generals, have no statues built in their honor. Several such persons are referred to in this book. Therefore we feel justified in claiming that our fieldwork has enriched humankind's historical and cul-tural legacy. What is more, by salvaging these histories through a combination of idea and practice, there has evolved an in-creased self-awareness and self-reliance on the part of base com-munities and hence their power for independent action. Thus participatory action-research has demonstrated in concrete cases its ability to further the progress of the grassroots rather than the vested interests of dominant groups.

This result has been achieved by laying greater emphasis on certain methods already used by historians and anthropologists and by applying some newer and unconventional techniques. These techniques have been referred to in Chapter 1. They operate within the heart of communities as essential ingredients for both scientific formulation and action motivation. Together they open doors for research and enable the base communities to recognize the value of their own knowledge and to allow it to flourish. These techniques help to explain and to sustain the immense capacity for resistance that characterizes popular life and culture as well as workers' struggles. As highlighted in our case studies, especially the African ones, the rediscovery of historical and cultural roots is an essential element in any effort to improve many depressed communities. These efforts fall within a frame of reference which so far has been largely out-of-bounds in institutions, but has now been rehabilitated and adopted as a theoretical alternative. It is called praxis.

Praxis was one of the first articulating concepts of the PAR movement. Proscribed as unscientific by positivists, it has from the beginning had the advantage of moving away from those schools where practice means technological manipulation or social engineering of humans, and instrumental control of natural and social processes. At first, following Hegel's dialectics and Marx's *Theses on Feuerbach* (as well as many Marxist thinkers), we emphasized the practical element in praxis so that for us praxis was a dialectical unit formed by theory and action in which action was cyclically determinant. Obviously, as work on contemporary hermeneutics by neo-Aristotelians has shown, such a definition of praxis is faulty because it does not include elements of practical knowledge, moral know-how and wise judgment (*phronesis*). Nevertheless, even with such partial understanding, it proved to have considerable utility for our initial work.[3]

One challenge presented by that interpretation was to prove whether theory can in fact be derived directly from action or in the course of action. This was attempted, with inconclusive results and some verticality, by Alexandre Bogdanov's *Proletkult* movement in the early days of the Soviet Union. Like him, we tried (also in vain) to build a "science of the proletariat" in Third World environments. Despite these failures, PAR techniques for the critical recovery of history and culture were still designed with a similar purpose in mind. Their application has proved encouraging in a number of cases (some of which are described here) by making possible some progress in people's struggles. Because of the complex nature of the problems involved, PAR techniques are now being developed on the basis of cultural and historical practical elements, including interdisciplinary and holistic principles as well as theoretical and technical knowledge. These approaches have been identified in this book as "praxiology" (Sethi 1987: 15-21).

Recent analyses have pointed to the need of distinguishing three movements in cultural-historical praxis, each of which has its own conditions and functions: (1) the investigative practice, which requires the usual care and discipline; (2) the ideological practice, which requires clarity and ability to understand and communicate; and (3) the political practice, which requires commitment, boldness and a utopian vision (Zamosc 1987: 37). PAR researchers attempt to connect the three movements by synergy in the field in the form of an action-reflection cycle, spiraling toward successive and more complex stages of theoretical discussion and practice. In each stage preconceptions and ad hoc statements are ventilated. This is difficult work because it involves acquiring knowledge, practicing science and impelling transformation all at the same time. In such a theory-action context, the mere asking of a question in the field carries with it a commitment to act: it spurs movement, much as was Marx's early intention with his labor questionnaire in 1880.

The combining of analysis and practice on the march requires outside researchers to adopt new or unusual roles. They may be expected by base communities to be ideologues and charismatic politicians as well as good historians and sociologists—"an impossible, self-defeating task!" say the critics. Faced with this dilemma, outside researchers usually insist that their most effective contribution still is their scientific and technical know-how, rather than any attempts on their part to replace local actors in the communities' political struggles. These researchers in turn would like to see local protagonists inspired and guided by personal involvement in the research effort. The scientific legitimacy of the participatory action-research is confirmed by this difficult balance between theory and practice. In this way the researcher-activist helps to modify and explain existing ideological, often alienating, representations through scientific knowledge as a liberating agent. Researchers may be tempted to subordinate their action research to the immediate needs of grassroots activists but, as illustrated in this book, this may not prove to be an insurmountable obstacle.

Obviously since our cultural-historical praxis requires wise judgment, commitment to people's struggles and insertion into social processes, it offers clear advantages in improving the lot of base communities over classical methods of doing detached research based on dissimulation and simple empathic attitudes. It should be observed that, as far as we know, there are no other ways except through participatory action-research to work successfully and responsibly in these dynamic, conflicting or processual conditions. The Ayacucho case presented by Gianotten and de Wit is eloquent enough, as are the African cases in which attempts have been made to articulate people's own praxis and culture (like the concept of *amalima* in Zimbabwe). PAR methodology appears to be the most effective way of building "knowledge democracy" today.

Convergences

A quick review is given in this section of recent intellectual and theoretical convergences between participatory action-research and other schools of thought (excluding liberation theology) in regard to remaking knowledge in the context of action.

The critical education group has been developing new pedagogical theories, like those introduced by John Elliott, Ivan Illich and Paulo Freire, with important social expressions. These include: the Ford Teaching Project in the United Kingdom, Global Learning in Canada, the Center for International Education and the Participatory Research Center at the University of Massachusetts-Amherst, Popular Education in Latin America and various experiences in Africa. Two important additions to this movement, although somewhat confusing and contradictory, came in 1981 in the form of publications by the Non-Formal Education Services at Michigan State University (NFE 1981), and the School of Social Work at the University of Montreal with contributions from France, Belgium and Switzerland (*Revue* 1981). Publications of both institutions have expressed support for action-research. Further recognition has come from the Australian educational action-research group, which recommends a participatory, collective approach to planning (Kemmis and McTaggart 1988), and proposals for "collaborative" or emancipatory action-research (Carr and Kemmis 1986: 5, 224).

PAR has benefited greatly from the examination of development projects undertaken by a number of economists anxious to restore economics to its human foundations, and to apply participatory principles in socioeconomic planning (Max-Neef 1982; Fuglesang and Chandler 1986; Hirschman 1984; Lutz and Lux 1988).

In Bratislava, Czechoslovakia, an interdisciplinary center has been founded to examine the relations between active social learning and anticipatory behavior and to mobilize social groups with the guiding concept of "Problem-Oriented Participative Forecasting (POPF)." It is expected that with this method common people would eventually be able to carry out forecasting themselves (Gal and Fric 1987).

Anthropologists have turned to aspects of agricultural life and to a "supportive social anthropology" that "assures the perspective of oppressed groups in a process of change" (Colombres 1982; Hernández 1987). Likewise, a few important historians have reconsidered "popular versions" of events and "peoples without history" (Wolf 1982; Ziegler 1983).

Some ethnologists are approaching indigenous and local cultures with a participative philosophy and suggesting that popular movements be redefined, bearing in mind the pluriethnic nature of national societies. Thus they go beyond anthropologist Sol Tax (with his detached observer brand of "action-anthropology"), and C. Levi-Strauss and D. Lewis (Stavenhagen 1988: 341-353; Bonfil Batalla 1981). Others are engaged in organizing "participatory communal museums," as in Mexico.

Among sociologists, Alain Touraine's method of "sociological intervention" (1978) comes close to PAR in its attempt to bridge the gap between research and action. In discussing social movements, he advises investigators to work with them as mediators, undertaking collective research with their actors but avoiding any deeper or open involvement or commitment. Hence this method is reminiscent of the detached participant-observer technique. Touraine, however, like us, emphasizes the contradictory nature of social processes, rejects traditional sociological surveys and group dynamics and favors the building of broader and more direct types of democracy.

Rural sociologists are also reviving the problem-solving orientation of their discipline, as first conceived in the 1920s, thereby coming closer to PAR. The heretofore fringe contributions of veteran researchers like T. R. Batten ("non- directive approach"), Irwin Sanders ("social reconnaissance") and Harold Kaufman ("the action approach") are now respectfully heeded (Fear and Schwarzweller 1985: xi-xxxvi). "Trust/political validity is as important as scientific validity"; this once heterodox principle is now recommended for applying "action research in community development." This qualitative, participatory recovery of rural sociology has been useful in studying farming systems (low external input agriculture), poverty/hunger indicators, environmental management and farm-output performance and is seen as a more comprehensive "sociology of agriculture," "alternative agriculture" or even "alternative society." Similar ideas are being employed in the Sahel by agriculture students who engage in "recherche-formation-action" with peasants to defend the fertility of sub-Saharan soils (ENDA 1987).

The psycho-social school of Kurt Lewin (1946), the first to introduce the concept of action-research in the 1940s in the United States and from which we took our first label, is now also in the convergent trend. We had deviated from this school when the "militant" or "committed" component was stressed and later on with the broader participation element of PAR. Lewin's work on the whole expressed preoccupations similar to PAR's (on theory/practice, social use of science, language and pertinence of information), but shortly after his death his followers reduced the fuller implications of Lewin's insights by linking them mainly to small-group processes (e.g., in industrial management) and clinical approaches (e.g., in veterans' rehabilitation). By 1970 the implicit value-loaded dilemmas of the Lewinians became clear (Rapoport 1970), but this did not deter them from forming the present Organization-Development school of action-research that has gone into community work, educational systems and organizational change. In the early 1980s there were efforts to use what was referred to already as a method of "participative action-research."

In recent self-criticisms, however, they admit that Organization-Development is unidimensional, fails to advance social knowledge of any consequence and reinforces and perfects the status quo (Cooperrider and Srivasta 1987). They recommend two ways of overcoming such failures: to develop a "metatheory of sociorationalism," which would include moral values and a "vision of the good," and to practice an "appreciative mode of inquiry" as a way of "living with and directly participating in the varieties of social organization we are compelled to study." It is readily seen that this school, perhaps through osmotic intellectual communication, has moved close to PAR, now re- baptized as "appreciative inquiry," with praxiology paraphrased as "sociorationalism."

More recently, there has appeared in Great Britain the "cooperative experiential inquiry" group that proposes to do research "*with* and *for* people rather than *on* people" (Reason 1988), as we have done in PAR from the beginning. Inspired by humanistic psychology, this trend criticizes the mechanical and reductionist scientific world view, calls for participatory and holistic knowing and recognizes PAR as one of its "schools." Unfortunately, these colleagues have preferred to experiment in artificial workshops seen "as a learning community" in order to "make sense" out of data, without giving enough attention to action in real contexts as we do in PAR. Of course, our experiences cannot be tied only to the developmental discourse and micro solutions ("safer stoves for cooking," the cited case in Reason 1988: 13, 224), as this group has suggested. And in 1988 in Leeds, a group of university professors from England and the United States concerned with the lack of critical analyses in their milieux decided to form a "transformative research network"(!), which sought to respect "the rights of those involved in the research to be active and informal participant" --quite a belated but welcome "discovery."

On Paradigms

Perhaps the theoretical positions of these schools and groups would become clearer if cooperative and appreciative inquirers, sociological interventors and mediators, alternative rural sociologists and agronomists, organization/development scholars, participative forecasters, transformative researchers and other critical colleagues gave due recognition to PAR philosophy and techniques for earlier attempts (since 1968 in the Third World especially) to both produce and remake science and knowledge. As we have seen, many of them have come close to PAR. They differ, however, in one important respect: their open search for new paradigms in the social sciences.

There are reasons to believe that winds of change are occurring in science in general, and not only in the social disciplines, so that different research priorities and concerns are the order of the day. The flavor and ambience of the scientific task per se has changed dramatically during the past decade, as witnessed by the seminal work of scholars like Capra (1982, 1988), Berman (1981), Churchman (1979), Hawking (1988) and the "chaos" non-linear physicists (Gleick 1987)—all of whom emphasize holistic philosophy, relativist knowledge, interdisciplinary descriptive methods, intuition, daily life phenomena and the human scale.

These trends have led some researchers, including a few PAR practitioners, to think in terms of new paradigms. Such colleagues as Heinz Moser (1975, 1978) have claimed that looking at the flip-side of the coin of knowledge through PAR is in fact a step toward building a new paradigm. But we are more circumspect today. Moser's affirmation would hold only if the metaphor of the two-sided coin corresponded to the actual situation. There is good reason to believe, as many scholars do, that we are facing a more complex reality better described as a set of many-sided dice. So the participatory approach to producing and remaking knowledge would go so far as to accept the general epistemic change in the overall nature of its search, short of claiming that PAR is a new paradigm or is building one on purpose. As mentioned in many parts of this book, we insist on considering our work as an open-ended process.

Moreover, in terms of Kuhnian principles, we hesitate to become self-appointed watchdogs of the new knowledge to decide what is scientific and what is not. It would mean playing the same game of intellectual superiority and technical control that we have been challenging in the academic world. Perhaps we should be content to follow Foucault (1980) and develop a more modest conceptual systematization of heretofore "subjugated knowledges," as a more stimulating and creative task.

Our present most important practical challenge is to respond to the need of the common people to articulate in social movements, along with the new knowledge, the necessary political struggles for justice and progress. This challenge requires a renewed commitment to change for the very same ideals that gave PAR its original *raison d'être*. The circle is closing. By retaking and redefining our iconoclastic origins, we are discovering once more the pertinence of participatory action-research to the transformation of our societies into a more satisfactory and less violent world.

NOTES

1. Cf. Macpherson (1977: 94, 98) and his thesis that "the main problem about participatory democracy is not how to run it but how to reach it." It is significant that this complex process of people's self-reliance has led to the organization of movements instead of new political parties, and that the procedure adopted has been from the base upwards and from the peripheries toward the center rather than the opposite, as has usually been the case with traditional parties, including those of the Marxist left. The resulting "hammocks," networks, social movements and self-reliance-promoting organizations, with evident political effects in constructing people's power, may be defined as collective efforts to redress abuse, neglect or evil from the state establishments and old political parties.

2. It so happens that "awakening" is the meaning for "development" in an African language, but it is more suitable to describe PAR goals as well as the ethos and pathos of the next century. The recent European trend to revive the provinces and autonomous regions, so evident in Spain, Italy, Belgium, France, Yugoslavia, the Soviet Union and other countries, has been a boon to participatory action-research efforts in Third World nations, where central autocracies have benefited from, and vegetated on, obsolete territorial divisions. There has been a surge of decentralizing measures and restructuring proposals based on a combination of ecological, economic and cultural variables (in Nicaragua, Colombia, Ecuador, Costa Rica, etc.), but much sustained effort is still needed to support local autonomies and people's self-reliant expressions. The work of such nineteenth century philosophical anarchists as P.J. Proudhon and Peter Kropotkin has been useful insofar as they understood the dangers of vertical and authoritarian systems in Europe and Siberia, and proposed ways of limiting abusive central powers (cf. Clastres 1987). Social historians and geographers like Fernand Braudel have also given impulse to the movement for regional autonomy and identity.

Interest on the part of PAR activists on the subject of the region was initially tied to the Marxist concept of social formation, then moved on to dependence theories and finally settled on concrete description and interpretation of local realities for purposes of cultural resistance and popular mobilization.

3. As is known, the *Theses on Feuerbach*, especially numbers II and XI, allowed some Marxists like G. Gentile to articulate a "philosophy of practice" (praxis), and Lenin, Mao Tsetung, Gramsci and Lukacs developed ideas toward the same end. Yet in PAR we still feel a lack of a "methodology of praxis" as such, unless such a method is put in terms of the synergistic elements of action-research which have been tried in our countries, as described here. Jürgen Habermas (1974) postulates the philosophy of history as a guide to praxis. The work of Habermas and other members of the Frankfurt School of Critical Theory, confirmed many of our concepts. But at the time of formulating them we were unaware of their thinking. For the hermeneutical approach, see Heller (1989), and especially H.G. Gadamer's classic *Truth and Method* (1982). Useful pertinent comments may be found also in Bernstein (1988: 30-49, 109-169).

REFERENCES AND
FURTHER READING

REFERENCES

AFL-CIO, Food and Beverage Trades 1984. *Manual of Corporate Investigation.* Washington D.C.: AFL-CIO.

Arizpe, Lourdes 1978. "Comentario a Himmelstrand" in Symposio Mundial de Cartagena, *Crítica y política en ciencias sociales.* Bogotá: Punta de Lanza, I, pp. 199-208.

Bakhtin, Mikhail et al. 1986. *Essays and Dialogues on His Work.* Chicago: University of Chicago Press.

Berman, Morris 1981. *The Reenchantment of the World.* Ithaca: Cornell University Press.

Bernstein, Richard J. 1988. *Beyond Objectivism and Relativism: Science, Hermeneutics and Praxis.* Philadelphia: University of Pennsylvania Press.

Bonfil Batalla, Guillermo 1981. *Utopía y revolución: el pensamiento político contemporáneo de los indios en América Latina.* Mexico: Nueva Imagen.

Borja, Jodi 1986. "Participación para qué?" *Revista foro* (Bogotá), I, 1, pp. 26-32.

Brandão, Carlos Rodrígues 1983. "La participación de la investigación en los trabajos de educación popular en el Brasil" in G. Vejarano (ed.), *La investigación participativa en América Latina.* Mexico: CREFAL, pp. 89-110.

Capra, Fritjof 1982. *The Turning Point.* New York: Simon & Schuster.

_____ 1988. *Uncommon Wisdom: Conversations with Remark-*

able People. New York: Simon & Schuster.

Carr, Wilfred and Stephen Kemmis 1986. *Becoming Critical: Education, Knowledge and Action Research*. Barcombe: The Falmer Press.

Chambers, Robert 1983. *Rural Development: Putting the Last First*. London: Longman Press.

Churchman, C. West 1979. *The Systems Approach and Its Enemies*. New York: Basic Books.

Clastres, Pierre 1987. *Society Against the State*. New York: Zone Books.

Colombres, Adolfo 1982. *La hora del bárbaro: bases para una antropología social de apoyo*. Mexico: Premia Editores.

Cooperrider, David L. and S. Srivastva 1987. "Appreciative Inquiry in Organizational Life," *Research in Organizational Change and Development*, I, pp. 129-169.

Darcy de Oliveira, R. and M. Darcy de Oliveira 1982. "The Militant Observer: A Sociological Alternative" in Budd Hall, A. Gillette and C. Tandon (eds.), *Creating Knowledge: a Monopoly? Participatory Research in Development*. New Delhi: Participatory Research Network Series 1, pp. 41-60.

Del Campo, Salustiano et al. 1976. *Diccionario de ciencias sociales*. Madrid: Instituto de Estudios Políticos and UNESCO.

Derickson, Alan 1983. "Down Solid: The Origins and Development of Black Lung Insurgency," *Journal of Public Health Policy* (March), pp. 25-44.

De Silva, G.V.S., Niranjan Mehta, Md. Anisur Rahman and Ponna Wignaraja 1979. "Bhoomi Sena: A Struggle for People's Power," *Development Dialogue* (Uppsala), II, pp. 3-70.

    A classic study that focuses on awareness-building in action among Indian peasants and the difficult role of committed intellectuals.

Draper, Hal 1977. *Karl Marx's Theory of Revolution: State and Bureaucracy, Vol. I*. New York: Monthly Review Press.

ENDA 1987. *Pour une recherche-formation-action sur la fertilité des sols*. Dakar: ENDA.

Escobar, Arturo 1987. *The Invention of Development*. University of California, Santa Cruz, Ph.D. thesis.

Esteva, Gustavo 1987. "Regenerating People's Space," *Alternatives*, XII, pp. 125-152.

    A pointed criticism of development policies with an alternative view inspired from the standpoint of involvement with grassroots "hammocks."

Fals-Borda, Orlando 1970. *Subversion and Development: The Case of Latin America*. Geneva: Foyer John Knox.

_____ 1979. "Investigating Reality in Order to Transform It: The Colombian Experience," *Dialectical Anthropology*, IV, 1 (March), pp. 33-55.

A detailed analysis of a participatory action-research experience among peasants during their struggle for land in a northern region of Colombia between 1972 and 1974.

_____ 1981. "Science and the Common People," *Journal of Social Studies* (Dacca), 11.

_____ 1982. "Participatory Research and Rural Social Change," *Journal of Rural Co-Operation*, X, 1, pp. 25-40.

_____1987. "The Application of Participatory Action-Research in Latin America," *International Sociology*, II, 4 (December), pp. 329-347.

_____ 1988a. *Knowledge and People's Power: Lessons with Peasants in Nicaragua, Mexico and Colombia*. New Delhi and New York: Indian Social Institute and New Horizons Press.

Utilizing the comparative approach, this collective book systematizes some of the main PAR methodological findings.

_____ 1988b. "Aspectos críticos de la política de participación popular," *Análisis político* (Bogotá), 2 (September), pp. 84-91.

_____ 1989. "Movimientos sociales y poder político," *Análisis político* (Bogotá), 8 (November), pp. 49-58.

Fear, Frank A. and H. K. Schwarzweller 1985. *Research in Rural Sociology and Development, II—Focus on Community*. London: JAI Press.

Feyerabend, Paul 1987. *Farewell to Reason*. London: Verso.

Fivaz, Roland 1989. *L'ordre et la volupté: essai sur la dynamique esthétique dans les arts et dans les sciences*. Lausanne: Presses Polytechniques Romandes.

Foucault, Michel 1980. *Power/Knowledge*. New York: Pantheon Books.

Freire, Paulo 1982. "Creating Alternative Research Methods: Learning to Do It By Doing It" in Budd Hall, A. Gillette and R. Tandon (eds.), *Creating Knowedge: A Monopoly? Participatory Research in Development*. New Delhi: Participatory Research Network Series 1, pp. 29-37.

Fuglesang, Andreas and D. Chandler 1986. *Participation as*

Process: What We Can Learn from Grameen Bank. Oslo: NORAD.

Gadamer, H.G. 1982. *Truth and Method.* New York: Continuum.

Gal, Fedor and Pavol Fric 1987. "Problem-Oriented Participative Forecasting: Theory and Practice," *Futures* (December), pp. 678-685.

Galeano, Eduardo 1978. *Las venas abiertas de América Latina.* Mexico: Siglo XXI.

Garfinkel, Harold 1967. *Studies in Ethno-methodology*, Englewood Cliffs, New Jersey: Prentice Hall.

Gaventa, John and Billy D. Horton 1981. "A Citizens' Research Project in Appalachia, USA," *Convergence* (Toronto), XIV, 3.

Gianotten, Vera and Ton de Wit 1985. *Organización campesina: el objeto político de la educación popular y la investigación participativa.* Amsterdam: CEDLA, Latin American Studies 30.

_____ and H. de Wit 1985. "The Impact of Sendero Luminoso on Regional and National Politics in Peru" in D. Slater (ed.), *The State and the New Social Movements in Latin America.* Amsterdam: CEDLA, Latin American Studies 29.

Gleick, James 1987. *Chaos: Making a New Science.* New York: Viking.

Guha, Ramachandra 1988. "The Alternative Science Movement: An Interim Assessment," *Lokayan Bulletin* (New Delhi), VI, 3 (May-June), pp. 7-26.

Habermas, Jürgen 1974. *Theory and Practice.* Boston: Prentice.

_____ 1984. *The Theory of Communicative Action, I.* Boston: Beacon Press.

Hall, Budd L. 1978. *Creating Knowledge: Breaking the Monopoly— Research Methods, Participation and Development.* Toronto: International Council for Adult Education.

_____ 1981. "El conocimiento como mercancía y la investigación participativa" in Francisco Vío Grossi, V. Gianotten and T. de Wit (eds.), *La investigación participativa en América Latina.* Pátzcuaro, Mexico: CREFAL, pp. 41-50.

Hawking, Stephen W. 1988. *A Brief History of Time.* New York: Bantam Books.

Heller, Agnes 1984. *Everyday Life.* London: Routledge and Kegan Paul.

_____ 1989. "From Hermeneutics in Social Science Toward a Hermeneutics of Social Science," *Theory and Society*, 18, 3 (May), pp. 291-322.

Hernández, Isabel 1987. "La investigación participativa y la antropología social de apoyo: dos paradigmas emergentes en América Latina," Buenos Aires, manuscript.

Hirschman, Albert O. 1984. *Getting Ahead Collectively: Grassroots Experiences in Latin America*. Elmsford, New York: Pergamon Press.

Huntington, Samuel P. and J. M. Nelson 1976. *No Easy Choice: Political Participation in Developing Countries*. Cambridge, Massachusetts: Harvard University Press.

Kapsoli, W. 1977. *Los movimientos campesinos en el Perú, 1879-1965*. Lima: Delva.

Kemmis, Stephen and Robin McTaggart 1988. *The Action Research Planner*. Geelong, Australia: Deakin University.
     A useful guide to PAR activities; especially designed for educators.

Kothari, Rajni 1984. "The Non-Party Political Process," *Economic and Political Weekly*, XIX, 5 (February).

KSSP (Kerala Sastra Sahithya Parishad) 1984. *Science as Social Activism*. Kerala: KSSP.
     A report on people's science movements in India in the early 1980s, as reported in a Trivandrum convention.

Kuhn, Thomas 1962. *The Structure of Scientific Revolutions*. Chicago: University of Chicago Press.

Landsberger, H. A. (ed.) 1978. *Rebelión campesina y cambio social*. Barcelona: Grijalbo.

LeBoterf, Guy 1981. *L'enquête participation en question: analyse d'une expérience, description d'une méthode et reflexions critiques*. Condé-sur-Noireau: Ch. Corlet.
     PAR examined in an orderly step-by-step way on the basis of Nicaraguan experiences.

Lévinas, Emmanuel 1974. *Humanismo del otro hombre*. Mexico: Siglo XXI.

Levine, Adeline Gordon 1982. *Love Canal: Science, Politics and People*. Lexington, Massachusetts: Lexington Books.

Lewin, Kurt 1946. "Action-Research and Minority Problems," *Journal of Social Issues*, 2, pp. 34-46.

Lindquist, Sven 1982. "Dig Where You Stand" in Paul Thompson and Natasha Burchardt (eds.), *Our Common History*. Atlantic Highlands, New Jersey: Humanities Press, pp. 322-340.

Lutz, Mark A. and Kenneth Lux 1988. *Humanistic Economics: The New Challenge*. New York: The Bootstrap Press.

Macpherson, C. B. 1977. *The Life and Times of Liberal Democracy.* Oxford: Oxford University Press.

Max-Neef, Manfred 1982. *From the Outside Looking In: Experiences in 'Barefoot Economics.'* Uppsala: Dag Hammarskjöld Foundation.

Ministerio del Trabajo-Universidad Nacional de Colombia 1986. *Niños y jóvenes trabajadores en Bogotá.* Bogotá: Universidad Nacional.

Moser, Heinz 1975. *Aktionsforschung als kritische Theorie der Sozialwissenschaften.* Münich: Kösel-Verlag.

Moser, Heinz and Helmut Ornauer (eds.) 1978. *Internationale Aspekte der Aktionsforschung.* Münich: Kösel-Verlag.

A rendition in German of some of the papers presented at the 1977 World Symposium on Action-Research held in Cartagena, Colombia—the first of its kind.

Nelkin, Dorothy and Michael Brown 1984. "Knowing About Workplace Risks: Workers Speak Out About the Safety of Their Jobs," *Science for the People*, XVI, 1, pp. 17-22.

NFE (Non-Formal Education Exchange) 1981. "Can Participation Enhance Development?" *The Exchange*, 20.

Nowotny, Helga et al. 1978. *Counter-Currents in the Sciences.* Dordrecht: Mouton.

Oakley, P. and D. Marsen 1984. *Approaches to Participation in Rural Development.* Geneva: International Labour Office.

A self-critical review of rural development policies in search of participatory alternatives.

Pateman, Carole 1970. *Participation and Democratic Theory.* Cambridge: Cambridge University Press.

Price, Richard 1983. *First Time: The Historical Vision of an Afro-American People.* Baltimore: Johns Hopkins University Press.

Rahman, Md. Anisur 1981. "Participation of the Rural Poor in Development," *Development: Seeds of Change* (Rome), 1.

_____ 1983. *Sarilakas: A Pilot Project for Stimulating Grassroots Participation in the Philippines.* Geneva: International Labour Office, Technical Co-operation Evaluation Report.

_____ (ed.) 1984. *Grass-Roots Participation and Self-Reliance: Experiences in South and South East Asia.* New Delhi: Oxford and IBH.

_____ 1985. "The Theory and Practice of Participatory Action-Research" in Orlando Fals-Borda (ed.), *The Challenge of Social Change.* London: Sage Publications, pp. 107-132.

A fundamental analytical paper on PAR that includes contemporary dilemmas and challenges for activists as well as for scientists.

_____ 1986. "Organizing the Unorganized Rural Poor (Bangladesh field notes, October-November)." Geneva: International Labour Office, mimeo.

_____ 1987a. "The Theory and Practice of Participatory Action-Research" in William R. Shadish, Jr. and Charles S. Reichart (eds.), *Evaluation Studies Review Annual*, XXII, pp. 135-160.

_____ 1987b. *Further Interaction with Grass-roots Organising Work*. Geneva: International Labour Office, mimeo.

Rapoport, Robert N. 1970. "Three Dilemmas in Action Resarch," *Human Relations*, XXIII, 6, pp. 499-513.

Reason, Peter (ed.) 1988. *Human Inquiry in Action: Developments in New Paradigm Research*. London: Sage Publications.

Restrepo, Luis Alberto 1988. "Los movimientos sociales, la democracia y el socialismo," *Análisis político* (Bogotá), 5 (September-December), pp. 56-67.

Revue Internationale d'Action Communautaire (Ecole de Service Social, Université de Montreal) 1981. "La recherche-action: enjeux et pratiques," 5/45 (Printemps).

Salazar, María Cristina 1987. *Una experiencia de investigación activa con menores trabajadores en Bogotá*. Lima: Centro Latinoamericano de Trabajo Social.

_____ 1988. "Child Labour in Colombia: Bogota's Quarries and Brickyards" in A. Bequele and Jo Boyden (eds.), *Combating Child Labour*. Geneva: International Labour Office.

Sethi, Harsh 1987. *Refocussing Praxis*. Colombo/New Delhi: PIDA and SETU-Lokayan.

Simposio Mundial de Cartagena 1978. *Crítica y política en ciencias sociales*. Bogotá: Punta de Lanza.

A most important compilation of PAR experiences and reflection which resulted from an international symposium held in Cartagena, Colombia, in 1977. This event marked the recognition of the world dimension of the PAR movement.

Stavenhagen, Rodolfo 1988. *Derecho indígena y derechos humanos en América Latina*. México: El Colegio de México and Instituto Interamericano de Derechos Humanos.

Tilakaratna, S. 1985. *The Animator in Participatory Rural Development: Some Experiences from Sri Lanka*. Geneva: International

Labour Office, WEP Working Paper 10/WP 37.

_____ 1987. *The Animator in Participatory Rural Development: Concept and Practice*. Geneva: International Labour Office, WEP Technical Cooperation Report.

A significant addition to the field viewed from actual training of activists in South and Southeast Asia.

Todorov, Tzvetan 1982. *La conquête de l'Amérique, la question de l'autre*. Paris: Editions du Seuil.

Touraine, Alain 1978. *La voix et le regard*. Paris: Editions du Seuil.

UNRISD (United Nations Research Institute for Social Development) 1981. *Dialogue about Participation*. Geneva: UNRISD.

Pertinent proposals on peoples' participation presented by Andrew Pearse on the basis of his Latin American experience. The first number of an influential series.

Vanek, Jaroslav 1971. *The Participatory Economy*. Ithaca: Cornell University Press.

Van Heck, B. 1979. *Participation of the Poor in Rural Organizations*. Rome: FAO-ROAP.

Vío Grossi, Francisco, Vera Gianotten and Ton de Wit (eds.) 1988. *Investigación participativa y praxis rural*. Santiago: CEAAL.

Wainwright, Hilary and Dave Elliott 1982. *The Lucas Plan: A New Trade Unionism in the Making?* London: Allison & Busby.

Wolf, Eric 1969. *Peasant Wars of the Twentieth Century*. New York: Harper & Row.

_____ 1982. *Europe and the People without History*. Berkeley: University of California Press.

Zamosc, Leon 1987. "Campesinos y sociólogos: reflexiones sobre dos experiencias de investigación activa en Colombia" in Foro por Colombia, *La investigación-acción en Colombia*. Bogotá: Foro por Colombia and Punta de Lanza.

An insightful analysis and comparison of two PAR rural experiences in Colombia, with a pertinent theoretical discussion.

Ziegler, Jean 1984. *Les rebelles: contre l'ordre du monde*. Paris: Editions du Seuil.

FURTHER READING

Almas, Reidar 1988. "Evaluation of a Participatory Development Project in Three Norwegian Rural Communities," *Community Development Journal*, XXIII, 1 (March), pp. 26-32.

Barbedette, L. (ed.) 1973. *Enquête et planification du développement: l'enquête-participation, méthodes pour l'action*. Douala: Institut Panafricaine pour le Développement, Document 10, 1978.

Bhaduri, A. and Md. Anisur Rahman 1982. *Studies in Rural Participation*. New Delhi: Oxford and IBH.

Bhasin, Kamla 1978. *Breaking Barriers: A South Asian Experience*. Bangkok and Paris: FAO.

Boudon, Raymond 1988. "Common Sense and the Human Sciences," *International Sociology*, III, 1 (March), pp. 1-22.

Brandão, Carlos Rodrigues 1981. *Pesquisa participante*. São Paulo: Editora Brasiliense.

Castillo, G.T. 1983. *How Participatory Is Participatory Development?* Manila: Institute of Development Studies.

Cernea, Michael M. 1983. *A Social Methodology for Community Participation in Local Investments*. Washington: IBRD.

Consejo de Educación de Adultos de América Latina (CEAAL) 1989. *Investigación participativa: Cuarto Seminario Latinoamericano*. Santiago de Chile: CEAAL.

_____ 1990. *Des de adentro: la educación popular vista porsus practicantes*. Santiago de Chile: CEAAL.

An important self-review of popular education in Latin America, showing its practical and political implications for reconstructing democracy, with a detailed chapter on PAR's pertinence to educators.

Crapanzano, Vincent et al. 1986. "Personal Testimony: Narratives of the Self in the Social Sciences and the Humanities," *Items*, XL, 2 (June), pp. 25-30.

Delruelle-Vosswinkel, N. 1981. "La recherche-action: nouvelle paradigme de la sociologie?" *Revue de l'Institut de Sociologie*, 3, pp. 513-527.

Demo, Pedro 1986. *Participação é conquista: noções de política social participativa*. Fortaleza, Brazil: Universidade Federal do Ceará.

de Schutter, Anton 1981. *Investigación participativa: una opción metodológica para la educación de adultos*. Pátzcuaro, Mexico: CREFAL.

This illuminating book bridged the span between PAR and popular education in a time of crisis and search for practical alternatives among educators.

deVries, Jan 1980. *Science as Human Behavior: On the Epistemology of Participatory Research Approach*. Amersfoort, Holland: Studiecentrum.

Egger, Paul 1988. "Participatory Technology Development: Who Shall Participate?" Information Centre for Low External Input Agriculture, Leusden, Holland, manuscript.

Erasmie, Thor and F. Dubell (eds.) 1980. *Adult Education: Research for the People, Research by the People*. Linköping, Sweden: University of Linköping.

Fals-Borda, Orlando and Carlos R. Brandão 1987. *Investigación participativa*. Montevideo: Instituto del Hombre.

A discussion, taped in Buenos Aires, which touches on the epistemological bearings and origins of PAR in Colombia and Brazil and the consequences of commitment to the interviewed.

Fernandes, Walter (ed.) 1985. *Development with People*. New Delhi: Indian Social Institute.

Fernandes, Walter and Rajesh Tandon 1981. *Participatory Research and Evaluation: Experiments in Research as a Process of Liberation*. New Delhi: Indian Social Institute.

Gajardo, Marcela (ed.) 1985. *Teoría y práctica de la educación popular*. Pátzcuaro, Mexico: CREFAL, IDRC, PREDE.

Gaventa, John 1980. *Power and Powerlessness in an Appalachian Valley*. Urbana: University of Illinois Press.

Gould, Jeremy (ed.) 1981. *Needs, Participation and Local Development*. Helsinki: EADI Basic Needs Workshop.

Gran, Guy 1983. *Development by People*. New York: Praeger.

Grell, P. 1981. "Problematique de la recherche-action," *Revue de l'Institut de Sociologie*, 3, pp. 605-614.

Huizer, Gerrit 1989. *The Anthropology of Crisis: Participatory Action-Research and Healing Witchcraft*. Nijmegen, Holland: Third World Center, University of Nijmegen.

Humbert, C. and J. Merlo, 1978. *L'enquête concientisation*. Paris: INODEP, Harmattan.

International Council for Adult Education (ICAE) 1981. "Participatory Research: Development and Issues," *Convergence* (Toronto), XIV, 3.

Kassam, Yussuf and Kemal Mustafa (eds.) 1982. *Participatory Research: An Emerging Alternative Methodology*. Toronto: ICAE.

Marx, Karl 1968. *Theses on Feuerbach: Selected Works*. Moscow and London: Lawrence & Wishart.

McTaggart, Robin 1989a. *Principles for Participatory Action-Research*. Geelong, Australia: Deakin University, School of Education, Document 7/89.

_____ 1989b. *Action-Research for Aboriginal Pedagogy*. Geelong: Deakin University, School of Education, Document 2/89.

 A rare study of PAR applicability among aboriginal groups, in this case those of North-Central Australia.

Merrifield, Juliet 1989. *Putting Scientists in Their Place: Participatory Research in Environmental and Occupational Health*. New Market, Tennessee: Highlander Center.

Mustafa, Kemal 1979. *The Jipemoyo Project*. Dar-es-Salaam: African Regional Workshop.

Nichter, M. 1984. "Project Community Diagnosis: Participatory Research as First Step Toward Community Involvement in Primary Health Care," *Social Science and Medicine*, 19, 3, pp. 237-252.

Oquist, Paul 1978. "The Epistemology of Action-Research," *Development Dialogue* (Uppsala), 1.

 A paper originally presented at the Cartagena Symposium, the first to broach formal cognitive and philosophical issues in PAR.

Orefice, Paul 1985. "Adult Education in Gramsci and Participatory Research in Italy," *Ricerche pedagogiche* (Parma), 76/77, pp. 1-17.

Park, Peter 1989. "What Is Participatory Research? A Theoretical and Methodological Perspective," University of Massachusetts, Amherst, manuscript.

Pearse, Andrew and M. Stiefel 1979. *Inquiry into Participation: A Research Approach.* Geneva: UNRISD.

Programme on Participatory Organisations of the Rural Poor (PORP) 1988. *Promoting People's Participation and Self-Reliance.* Geneva: International Labour Office.

Punta de Lanza and Foro por Colombia 1987. *La IAP en Colombia: taller nacional.* Bogotá: Foro por Colombia.

Rudqvist, Anders 1981. *"Rosca" in the Peasant Movement, 1970-1975.* Uppsala: Department of Sociology, University of Uppsala.
     A well-documented evaluation of the early Colombian experience of PAR.

Rahnema, Majid 1989. "Power and Regenerative Processes in Micro-Spaces," Port-la-Galere, manuscript.

_____ 1990. "Participatory Action-Research: The 'Last Temptation of Saint' Development" *Alternatives*, XV, 2 (Spring), pp. 199-226.
     A polemical article underlining cooptation dangers for PAR and some alternatives in unstructured moral social movements of India.

Society for International Development 1983. *Grassroots Initiatives in Developing Countries and UNDP Project Planning and Implementation.* Rome: SID.
     One of a series of worthwhile attempts at assimilating PAR by international institutions.

Swantz, Marja Liisa 1980. *Rejoinder to Research: Methodology and the Participatory Research Approach.* Dar-es-Salaam: Ministry of Culture and Youth.

Swedner, Harald 1983. *Human Welfare and Action Research in Urban Settings.* Stockholm: Delegation for Social Research.

Tandon, Rajesh 1989. *Movement Towards Democratization of Knowledge.* New Delhi: Society for Participatory Research in Asia.

_____ 1988. "Social Transformation and Participatory Research," *Convergence* (Toronto), XXI, 2/3, pp. 5-14.

Thiollent, Michel 1985. *Metodología da pesquisa-ação.* São Paulo:

Cortéz Editora.

Touani, A.B. 1989. *Le rizo et le giza. Quel avenir? Conclusions d'une recherche-action*. Milano: Centro Studie Ricerche Africa, CER-FAP-FOCSIU.

United Nations University 1984. *People's Movements and Experiments: Report of a Meeting of South Asian Scholars*. Colombo: PIDA.

Vejarano M., Gilberto (ed.) 1983. *La investigación participativa en América Latina*. Pátzcuaro, Mexico: CREFAL.

Volpini, Domenico, A. del Lago and L. Wood 1988. *Participatory Action-Research in Primary Health Care Programmes*. Padova, Italy: CUAMM, University of Bologna and University of Nairobi.

Wignaraja, Ponna 1986. *Ten Years of Experience with Participatory Action-Research in South Asia: Lessons for NGO's and People's Organisations*. Colombo: PIDA.

Yopo, Boris 1981. *Metodología de la investigación participativa*. Pátzcuaro, Mexico: CREFAL.

Zevenbergen, William 1984. "Official Development Assistance and Grassroots Action: A Delicate Relationship," *Development: Seeds of Change* (Rome, SID), 2, pp. 60-62.

ABOUT THE CO-AUTHORS

Gustavo I. de Roux. Sociologist (Ph.D. Wisconsin); former director of EMCODES (Empresas de Cooperación para el Desarrollo); dean of the Faculty of Education, University of Valle, Cali, Colombia; and director of Fundación El Palenque, Cali; at present, consultant to Ministry of Public Health, Bogotá.

Ton de Wit. Dutch, based in Latin America since 1976. Rural sociologist with Ph.D. on the basis of research on peasant economy in the Andean part of Peru. Worked nine years in Peru and three in Nicaragua. Together with Vera Gianotten, wrote several books and numerous articles. Visiting professor of the Faculty of Social Sciences and Economy at the Catholic University of Peru in Lima.

Orlando Fals-Borda (Ph.D. Florida). Professor emeritus of sociology at the Institute of Political and International Studies, National University of Colombia, Bogotá; president of Latin American Council for Adult Education (CEAAL); awarded Kreisky and Hoffman Prizes; and author of several publications on people's participation and other subjects.

John Gaventa. Research coordinator at the Highlander Research and Education Center, New Market, Tennessee, and Assistant Professor of Sociology, University of Tennessee, Knoxville, USA; and author of books and articles on social participation.

Vera Gianotten. Dutch, working in Latin America since 1976. Rural sociologist with Ph.D. based on research of peasant organization in Peru. Worked nine years in Peru and three in Nicaragua. Wrote several books together with Ton de Wit on participatory research and numerous articles. Heads the Dutch Technical Cooperation Programme in Peru.

Sithembiso Nyoni. Sociologist and social worker from Zimbabwe, organizer and head of ORAP (Organisation of Rural Associations for Progress), Bulawayo, Zimbabwe.

Muhammad Anisur Rahman. Former professor of economics at the University of Dacca, Bangladesh; coordinator of the Programme on Participatory Organisations of the Rural Poor (PORP), Rural Employment Policies Branch, Employment and Development Department, International Labour Office (Geneva); and author of several publications on people's participation.

María Cristina Salazar. Sociologist (Ph.D. Catholic University); associate professor, National University of Colombia, Bogotá. Author of articles and books on rural social development, women and poverty, and child laborers in urban and rural areas. Currently engaged in PAR projects with adolescents in marginal urban areas.

S. Tilakaratna. Social scientist from Sri Lanka; research director at PIDA (Participatory Institute for Development Alternatives), Colombo, Sri Lanka; consultant for International Labour Office on rural participation questions and training.